kiddiwalks in

Hampshire and the New Forest

COUNTRYSIDE BOOKS
NEWBURY BERKSHIRE

First published 2010
© Jane Pitman 2010
Reprinted 2015, 2021

COUNTRYSIDE BOOKS
3 Catherine Road
Newbury, Berkshire

To view our complete range of books,
please visit us at
www.countrysidebooks.co.uk

ISBN 978 1 84674 177 7

Designed by Peter Davies, Nautilus Design
Produced through The Letterworks Ltd., Reading
Typeset by KT Designs, St Helens
Printed by The Holywell Press, Oxford

Contents

AREA MAP SHOWING LOCATION OF THE WALKS

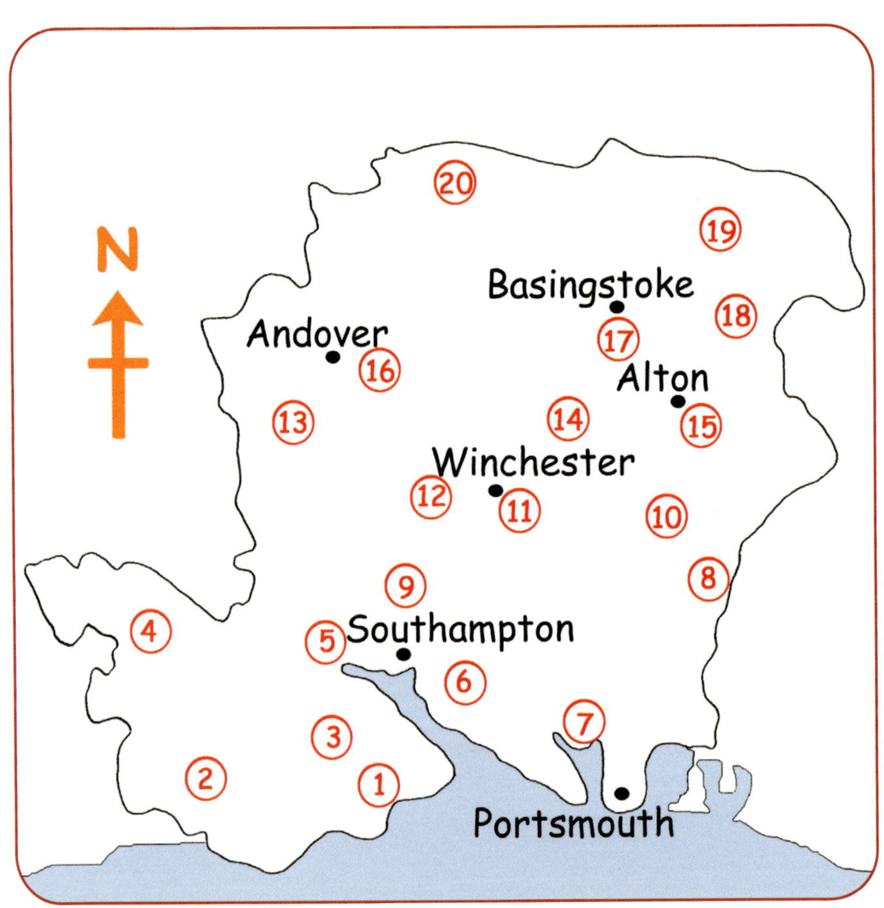

Contents

PUBLISHER'S NOTE

We hope that you obtain considerable enjoyment from this book; great care has been taken in its preparation. Although at the time of publication all routes followed public rights of way or permitted paths, diversion orders can be made and permissions withdrawn.

We cannot, of course, be held responsible for such diversion orders and any inaccuracies in the text which result from these or any other changes to the routes nor any damage which might result from walkers trespassing on private property. We are anxious though that all details covering the walks are kept up to date and would therefore welcome information from readers which would be relevant to future editions.

The simple sketch maps that accompany the walks in this book are based on notes made by the author whilst checking out the routes on the ground. They are designed to show you how to reach the start, to point out the main features of the overall circuit and they contain a progression of numbers that relate to the paragraphs of the text.

However, for the benefit of a proper map, we do recommend that you purchase the relevant Ordnance Survey sheet covering your walk. The Ordnance Survey maps are widely available, especially through booksellers and local newsagents.

Introduction

I have fond memories of country walks with my parents, spending many happy hours learning the names of plants and trees, trying to identify different types of birdsong and chasing butterflies in wildflower meadows – and I have continued to enjoy walking in the countryside ever since.

There is no shortage of safe and interesting places to take children for walks in Hampshire. Woodlands, for example, can be enjoyable at any time of the year: carpeted with bluebells in spring, offering a cool picnic spot in summer, concealing conkers among the fallen leaves in autumn, and displaying the first snowdrops in late winter. Do remember, though, that the paths through the woods can get muddy after wet weather so I would suggest that the youngsters are encouraged to wear their wellies on all but the driest of days.

If your children like feeding the ducks, take them along to Alresford or Whitchurch. Testwood Lakes Nature Reserve is a good place for bird watching, with two excellent hides and also wooden screens along the edge of the water where children can peep through holes to see the many different species that regularly visit the lakes. The RSPB recommend feeding ducks oats, salad, corn, or defrosted frozen peas, rather than bread, as it is closer to their natural diet.

The New Forest National Park is a wonderful landscape of coastal salt marshes, heath and ancient woodlands and is the perfect place for a quiet stroll and a picnic. If you're lucky, you might see ponies, donkeys, cattle, deer or pigs wandering in the open ground. Burley is a popular tourist destination in the forest, with a history of smugglers, witches and a dragon. From Castle Hill you get a wonderful view from an Iron Age hill fort, where an old smugglers' road can be seen snaking across the heath.

For more energetic excursions, the Iron Age hill forts of Danebury, St Catherine's Hill and Beacon Hill are ideal for a spot of climbing, playing imaginary battles on the ramparts, or flying kites on windy days, whilst adults can enjoy extensive views across the Hampshire countryside. All three hill forts are Sites of Special Scientific Interest, with chalk grassland habitats rich in wildlife, and St Catherine's Hill is part of East Hampshire's Area of Outstanding Natural Beauty.

For steam train enthusiasts, why not combine a pleasant stroll around the attractive Georgian town of Alresford with a trip to the station? The Watercress Line is a restored heritage steam railway, and runs special activity days for children during the summer months, including a trip on 'Thomas the Tank Engine'.

I have included three country parks, which all have picnic sites, easy access trails for pushchairs, nature or activity trails where children can search for wildlife, and also safe, well-equipped play areas where the youngsters can let off steam. Lepe Country Park, based on the Solent waterway, has historic D-Day remains to investigate on the beach and, when the tide is out, a hunt for crabs in rock pools and searching for shells are enjoyable pastimes.

I have really enjoyed my time researching these walks, watching excited children running up and down hills, feeding ducks, playing hide and seek among the trees and following nature trails in country parks, and I hope you have fun on these family outings, too.

Jane Pitman

New Forest ponies.

Acknowledgements

Thanks to Hampshire County Council Museums and Archives Service for permission to photograph an exhibition in the Curtis Museum, and I am grateful to all the families I met in Hampshire who kindly allowed me to take photographs as they enjoyed their walks.

Lepe Country Park

Two walks in one

Situated in the beautiful New Forest National Park, Lepe Country Park is a great place to take youngsters to let off steam. You can do either a short walk (see points 1 and 2) with younger children through a pretty wood in the conservation area, or you can take the older children along the beach (see points 3 and 4) to look at the D-Day remains, where thousands of troops left the Hampshire coast bound for Normandy in 1944. If you're feeling energetic, you can do both! If you are walking with a pushchair, you can take the easy access path to the observation point for views across the Dark Water estuary. Visit the information centre to pick up a free leaflet, which includes a map of the park (telephone: 023 8089 9108; website: www.hants.gov.uk/lepe).

Getting there *Leave the M27 at junction 2, signed to Hythe and Fawley. Take the A326 towards Fawley. At Holbury, follow signs for Blackfield and Lepe. Then follow the brown signs to Lepe.*

Length of walk Short walk ¾ mile; longer walk 1¾ miles; 2½ miles to combine the two.
Time About ¾ hour for the short walk and 1 hour for the longer walk.
Terrain The short walk has an easy access path to the observation point but after that there are steps up and down.

Buggies can be pushed from the top car park along to the beach.
Start/Parking The car park at the visitor centre where there are toilets. There are parking charges all year. The car park is divided into top and bottom and the walks start from the top car park (GR 456986).
Map OS Outdoor Leisure 22 New Forest.
Refreshments Take a picnic or visit the beachfront café and take-away, which serves hot and cold food, drinks and ice-creams (open daily from March to September, 10 am to 5 pm, and weekends only from October to March, 11 am to 4 pm).

◆ Background Notes ◆

The **remote village of Lepe**, known as Leope, Lupe and Leape in the past, was the perfect place to smuggle in contraband from France. Billy Coombes, the captain of a smuggling ship, was captured by Preventative Officers and hanged at Stone Point in the early 1800s.

In the **D-day landings**, Lepe was the major departure point for troops and vehicles on 6th June 1944. During the invasion the army had to be kept supplied and it was likely that as the German army retreated they would destroy suitable harbours. The solution was to build a floating Mulberry Harbour and tow it across to France (see 'Background Notes' Walk 3). To meet the constant need for fuel, a pipeline under the sea (PLUTO) was developed running from Lepe to the Isle of Wight and under the channel to France. This pipe supplied 172 million gallons of fuel.

Kiddiwalks in Hampshire & the New Forest

The Walk

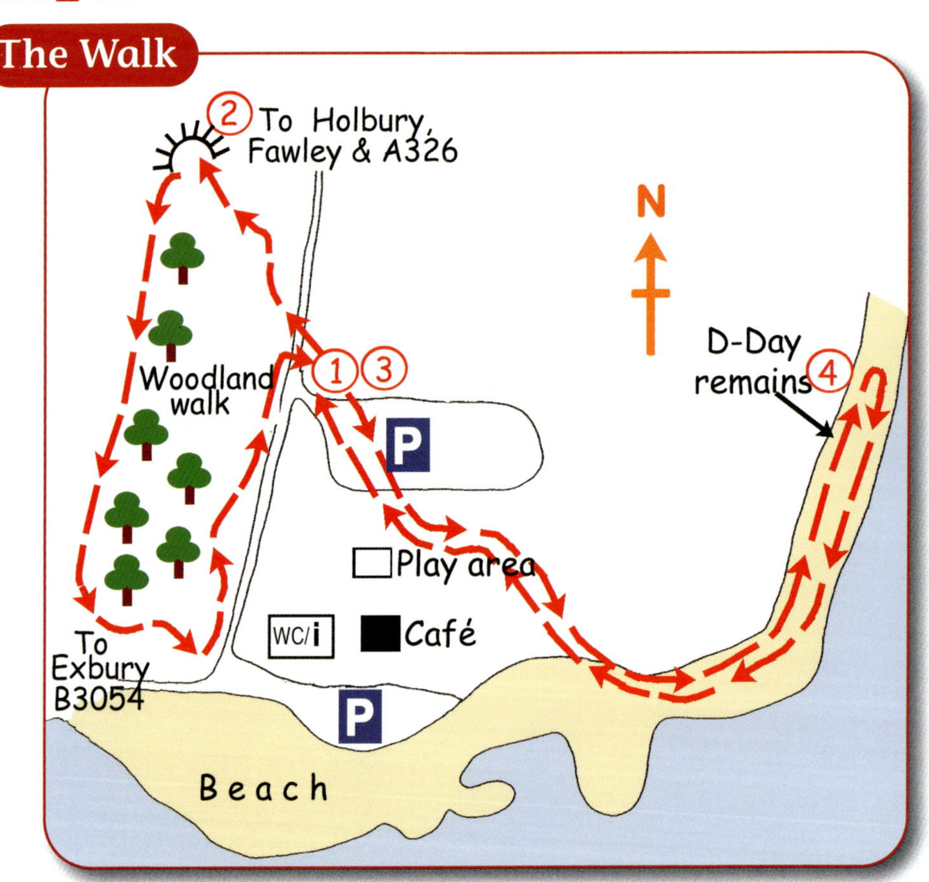

1 *To start the short walk, make your way to the entrance to the top car park. Cross Lepe Road with caution, and go through a gate into Lepe Point conservation area. This is now the start of the nature trail. Follow the gravel path and get the children to look out for posts where they can take brass rubbings of* animals and plants. Follow the path through a line of beech trees, past a pond on the left, and when you reach the observation point you can admire the view overlooking the Dark Water estuary.

2 To continue, take the path signed 'Woodland Walk'. Follow the path through the trees and then go down steps and continue along a wooden walkway. A little further on there is an interestingly shaped beech tree. Carry on as the path twists and turns, climb some brick steps and continue back to the gate. Cross the road to the car park.

3 *At this point you can start the longer walk.* Follow the right-hand edge of the car park and go past the children's play area and continue along the path with the sea to your right. Note the anchor next to a memorial dedicated to the men who gave their lives during the D-Day invasion of 1944. Continue along the gravel path, which eventually leads down onto the beach again. Carry on along the beach to an information board; this explains the history of wartime activity on the beach.

4 *On your return journey,* walk along the construction platforms for part of the way then return to the beach to retrace your steps back to the top car park. If you want to call in at the visitor centre, there are some steps next to the children's play area by the top car park which lead down to the lower car park. Turn right and the visitor centre, toilets and beach café can be found on the right.

A reminder of the D-Day landings of 1944.

1

◆ Fun Things to See and Do ◆

The shorter woodland walk has an **activity trail** that kids can follow, stopping at points along the way to learn about animals and plants that live in the park. A **nature trail booklet** and wax crayon for **brass rubbings** are available from the information centre for a small charge. There is a **well-equipped play area** near the top car park and a **wildflower meadow** that has an abundance of flowers and butterflies in the summer months.

The longer walk is full of history about the **D-Day landings**, which should appeal to older children, while younger ones will happily spend time **poking about in the sand** to see what treasures they can unearth and looking for **shells and hermit crabs** in the water edge pools when the tide is right out.

There are many **sea and shore birds** to watch out for all year round, including curlew, ringed plover, oystercatcher, pied wagtail, cormorant, grey heron and little egret. Winter visiting birds to see are dunlin, brent goose, grey plover and turnstone. The common tern is a summer visitor and if you're lucky you may catch a glimpse of the Mediterranean gull, a scarce visitor to Lepe, identified by its bright red bill.

Growing near the café are **Monterey pine trees**, originating from coastal California, which have pine cones that can be up to 50 years old. Look out for the hardy yellow horned-poppy, which thrives in the shingle, and the white flowers of sea campion, which prefers sandy areas.

Burley

Beware witches and man-eating dragons

A Coven of Witches in Burley.

Burley is a picturesque village in the New Forest and the perfect starting point for this peaceful walk to Castle Hill and the Iron Age hill fort where you can admire the views across Vales Moor and Strodgemoor Bottom. You can point out the remains of the ramparts to the children and keep an eye out for ponies wandering amongst the trees or across the moorland. Once back in the village you can browse in the range of interesting gift shops, have lunch in one of the traditional inns or enjoy a cream tea or delicious ice-cream in one of the many tea shops.

2

Getting there *From the A31 east of Ringwood follow the brown tourist signs to Burley, which will take you to the village centre.*

Length of walk 3½ miles.
Time 2 hours.
Terrain Minor roads, gravel tracks and woodland paths.
Start/Parking Park in the pay and display car park in Burley village (GR 212032).
Map OS Outdoor Leisure 22 New Forest.
Refreshments If you fancy a picnic, there are picnic tables on a grass area next to the car park. Alternatively, the following tea shops are in Burley village: the Burley Stores provides home-made meals and has a children's menu; the Old Farmhouse Tea Rooms and Restaurant is family-friendly, with plenty of outside seating. The White Buck is a five-minute drive from Burley and is set in 3 acres of woodland. It serves delicious food and is family friendly with an outside children's play area and log trail. Booking is advisable. Tel: 01425 402264 Website: www.whitebuckburley.co.uk.

1 Go through the gate by the information board at the end of the car park and walk between the gift shops along the Mall. At the road turn right and continue through the village along Ringwood Road. When you reach Clough Lane on the left, cross the

◆ Fun Things to See and Do ◆

The children will enjoy seeing the many **New Forest ponies** in Burley and as you walk across the moorland.

If you're feeling energetic, **bikes can be hired** from the Forest Leisure Cycle centre where you can follow easy access cycle routes through the woods, along a disused railway track and quiet country roads. In the summer months, enjoy a trip on a **horse-drawn wagonnette** along the forest lanes or take a **tractor and trailer ride** to see the red deer and their calves in Burley Deer Park.

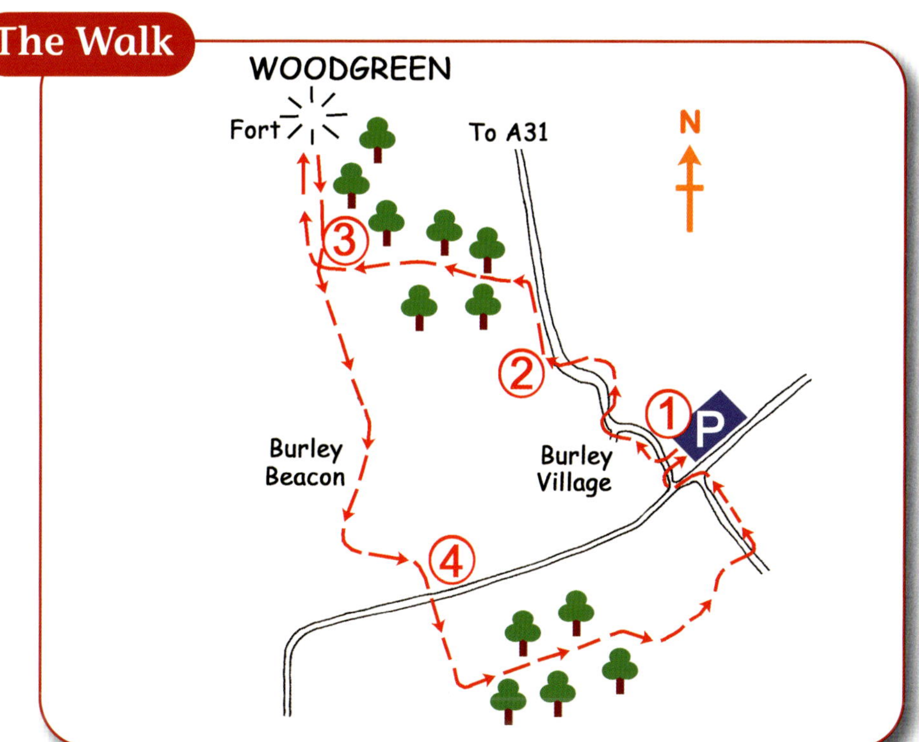

road with care, and go through a metal gate onto a footpath signed 'Burley Street'. Follow the metalled path up the hill then drop down again to the road.

2 Cross the road with caution and turn right. After a short distance turn left into Burley Hill House driveway. Go through the right-hand metal gate onto a footpath between fences. Continue up the hill through the wood.

3 Cross a stile and turn right at the gravel track. Continue for about ¼ mile and soon you will see the ramparts of the fort on either side of the track. There are splendid views from here. Retrace your steps back to the stile and continue ahead along the gravel track. A little further on is Burley Beacon, once said to be home of the man-eating Bisterne Dragon in the 15th century. A brave knight, Sir Maurice Berkeley, killed the dragon but unfortunately died during the fight.

4 When you reach the road, cross with care and take the path straight ahead between the field and the house. Carry on along this path for about ¼ mile. Keep the fence and embankment to your left when the path bears to the left and continues uphill through the wood. Keep ahead when the path becomes a lane and walk to the left of Moorhill House Hotel. Continue on the lane for about ½ mile and when you reach a gravel track turn right and continue to the road. Carefully cross the road, turn left and carry on down the hill to the village shops and car park.

A friendly cow in the New Forest.

◆ Background Notes ◆

Burley was a favourite **haunt for smugglers** in the 18th and 19th centuries. A path below the hill fort is an old smugglers' road that runs north from Vales Moor to Pickets Post. During renovations to the 17th-century Queen's Head inn, old coins, pistols and bottles were discovered in a cellar under the bar which may have been a hiding place for smugglers.

During the 1950s a white witch, **Sybil Leek**, lived in Burley and was often seen walking the streets with a pet jackdaw on her shoulder. She named one of the gift shops in the village 'A Coven of Witches' and her picture hangs beside a Jacobean fireplace inside the shop, which is still a thriving business today.

The **New Forest Centre in Lyndhurst** is a good place to learn all about life in the forest with interesting displays, including details of its fascinating history, and free colourings and quizzes for the children. Within the centre is the New Forest reference library, visitor information centre and a gift shop. For more information visit the website: www.newforestmuseum.org.uk or telephone 023 8028 3444.

Beaulieu

Down by the riverside

A yacht at anchor in the Beaulieu River.

This easy 4-mile walk is on level paths alongside the Beaulieu River, with a pleasant return journey through the woods. The picturesque village of Beaulieu lies in the heart of the New Forest, which became a National Park in 2005. The landscape of coastal salt marshes, mud flats, heath and ancient woodland is much the same today as it was 900 years ago, when William the Conqueror hunted wild deer and boar through the forest, and there is much wildlife to see. As well as this interesting circuit, you will find plenty of things to do in and around Beaulieu, where you can visit the abbey, Palace House and gardens, and the British National Motor Museum. Nearby is the 18th-century village of Buckler's Hard, which can be incorporated into the walk, with its Maritime Museum and historic cottage displays.

3

Getting there *Beaulieu lies between Bournemouth and Southampton on the B3054. From the M27, exit at junction 2 and follow the brown signs to Beaulieu.*

Length of walk 4 miles but add an extra mile if you continue to Bucklers Hard.

Time Allow 2 hours for the walk but you can easily spend the whole day here if you visit Bucklers Hard and the various sites in Beaulieu.

Terrain The paths are level and mostly gravel, with some wooden trackways by the river. Some of the riverside paths can be muddy after wet weather.

Start/Parking The pay and display car park in Beaulieu village (GR 387022).

Map OS Outdoor Leisure 22 New Forest.

Refreshments The Old Bakery Tea Rooms and the Montagu Arms Hotel in Beaulieu village are both child-friendly and there are several shops selling ice-creams.

1 From the car park take the gravel path, which passes an information board and tea rooms. Cross the road and continue on the gravel path, following the signs for Buckler's Hard. Go through a kissing gate and after a short while pass

◆ Fun Things to See and Do ◆

At the footbridge on point 2 of the walk, there is the perfect spot to play pooh sticks, a favourite game of Winnie the Pooh and his friends.

While strolling along beside the river, the children can count how many boats they see moored on the water and in the woods get them to look out for a wooden bungalow on stilts.

In Beaulieu High Street take a look at the shop selling collectable teddy bears, which is pushchair-friendly and has one teddy bear waiting for a cuddle from visitors!

The Walk

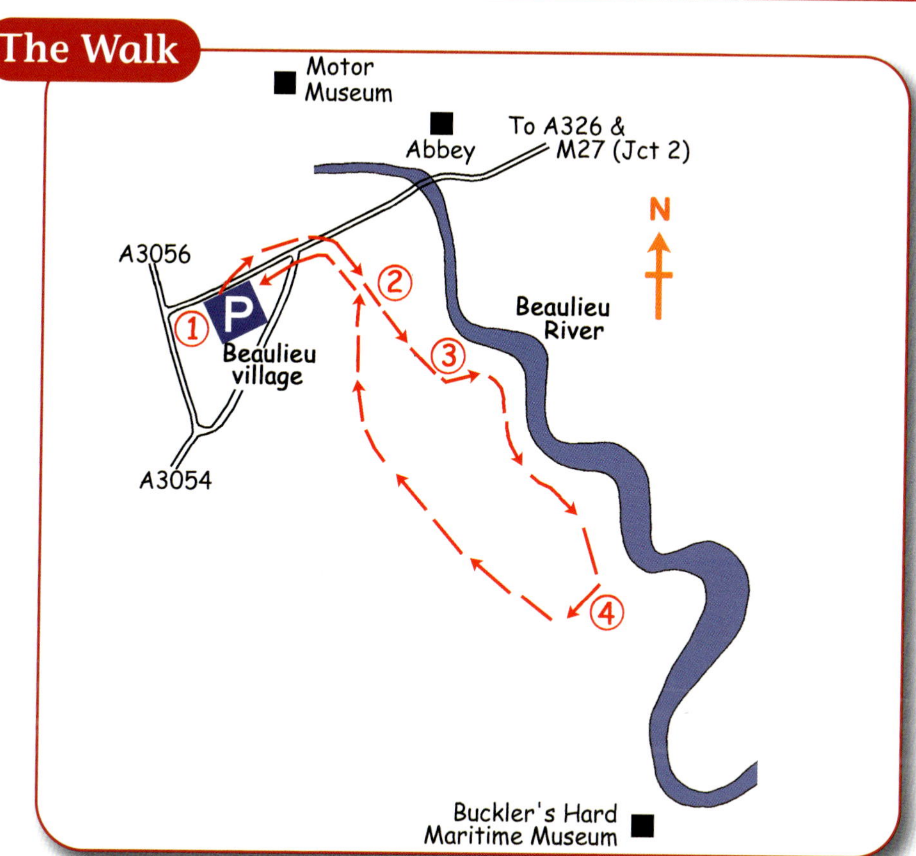

through a second kissing gate and turn right. Carry on to a wooden gate and continue to North Solent Nature Reserve.

2 After a short while you come to a footbridge. Keep following the signs for Buckler's Hard and when you reach a sign for 'Riverside Walk', turn left.

3 Continue alongside the Beaulieu River and follow the path over wooden trackways and footbridges. When the path splits, bear left over a wooden footbridge and continue beside the river. When you come to a seat, bear right away from the river and eventually you reach a junction of paths.

4 At this point you can turn left if you wish to visit Buckler's Hard, which is about another ½ mile further on. *To continue the walk,* turn right to stroll through the woods, rejoining the outward route at the sign for the riverside walk in point 2. Continue, following the signs back to Beaulieu village.

◆ Background Notes ◆

The village of **Buckler's Hard** started life as a port, trading sugar from the West Indies, and later developed a thriving shipbuilding industry where many naval warships were built for Admiral Nelson's fleet. In the Second World War, segments of the **Mulberry Harbour** were constructed here and towed across to Normandy in preparation for the D-Day landings. For more information visit www.bucklershard.co.uk or telephone 01590 616203.

The **Palace House** is the family home of the present Lord Montagu and his family, set in immaculate gardens overlooking the Beaulieu River. An example of a Gothic house, it was originally the Great Gatehouse to Beaulieu Abbey and has been extended twice, once in the 16th century then again in the 19th century. The Victorian kitchen garden still provides the house with seasonal vegetables, fruit and flowers. The vine house produces peaches, plums, apricots, dessert grapes and nectarines. At the **Palace House**, children can meet housemaids and a cook and butler, who provide a fascinating insight into life in a Victorian household

The **abbey**, founded in 1204 by Cistercian monks, has interesting wall hangings in the Domus, which at one time was used as a lay brothers' refectory. The hangings were designed and created by Lady Montagu and show scenes from medieval monastic life.

The **British National Motor Museum** has something for everyone – there is a secret army exhibition, the James Bond experience and over 250 historic motor vehicles including four world land speed record holders and Del Boy's Reliant Regal. Children will enjoy the remote control cars, mini car circuit and mini motor play trail. For more information visit www.beaulieu.co.uk or telephone 01590 612345.

Godshill Inclosure

Getting close to nature

The New Forest on a bright autumn day.

Whatever time of year you visit the New Forest National Park, there is always something to see and do. It is a wonderful place to observe wildlife within the different habitats of grassland, bog, ancient woodland and heather-covered moorland. In spring, just before the bluebells fill ancient woods in the Inclosures with their heady scent, see if you can spot the dainty nodding white flowers of wood anemone. In the summer months take a picnic to enjoy on the heath. In autumn, there is the fun of kicking fallen leaves along the paths leading through the woods at Castle Hill, the Iron Age hill fort, and watching squirrels burying nuts which they will later dig up to eat during the winter. Snowdrops are a wonderful sight in late winter, as are lesser celandine, with their bright yellow flowers, which herald the coming of spring.

4

Getting there *From the A338, when you reach Breamore take the turning for Woodgreen. Follow the lane to the village and fork right at the triangle. After about 1 mile you will see Godshill Wood car park on the left.*

Length of walk 3 miles.
Time Allow 2 hours.
Terrain Mostly level gravel paths, with some woodland paths. There is a gentle walk up Castle Hill to the viewpoint.
Start/Parking Godshill Wood car park, where there is free parking (GR 176160).

Map OS Outdoor Leisure 22 New Forest.
Refreshments The Horse and Groom in Woodgreen welcomes children and has a large beer garden. The Bat and Ball Inn, Salisbury Road, Breamore, is also a child-friendly pub. There is also a community shop in Woodgreen village, where you could purchase food to enjoy on a picnic in the forest.

1 Leave the car park from the far end, passing through a wooden gate, then bear left along the path through the wood. At the gravel track, turn left and

◆ Fun Things to See and Do ◆

As well as enjoying the sight of **New Forest ponies**, keep an eye out for **deer** among the trees – you might see fallow, roe, muntjac, Japanese sika and red deer. As you walk along the paths, watch out for **dung beetles and southern wood ants**. On the heath, colonies of **silver studded blue butterflies** are found in the summer months and, if you look among the gorse, you might spot a tiny bird, the **Dartford Warbler**. Also **stonechats** are frequently seen; listen out for their song, which sounds like two stones being knocked together. If you visit the open forest in October, you might be lucky to see the pigs that are turned out at this time of year. They eat green acorns, which are poisonous to the ponies.

The Walk

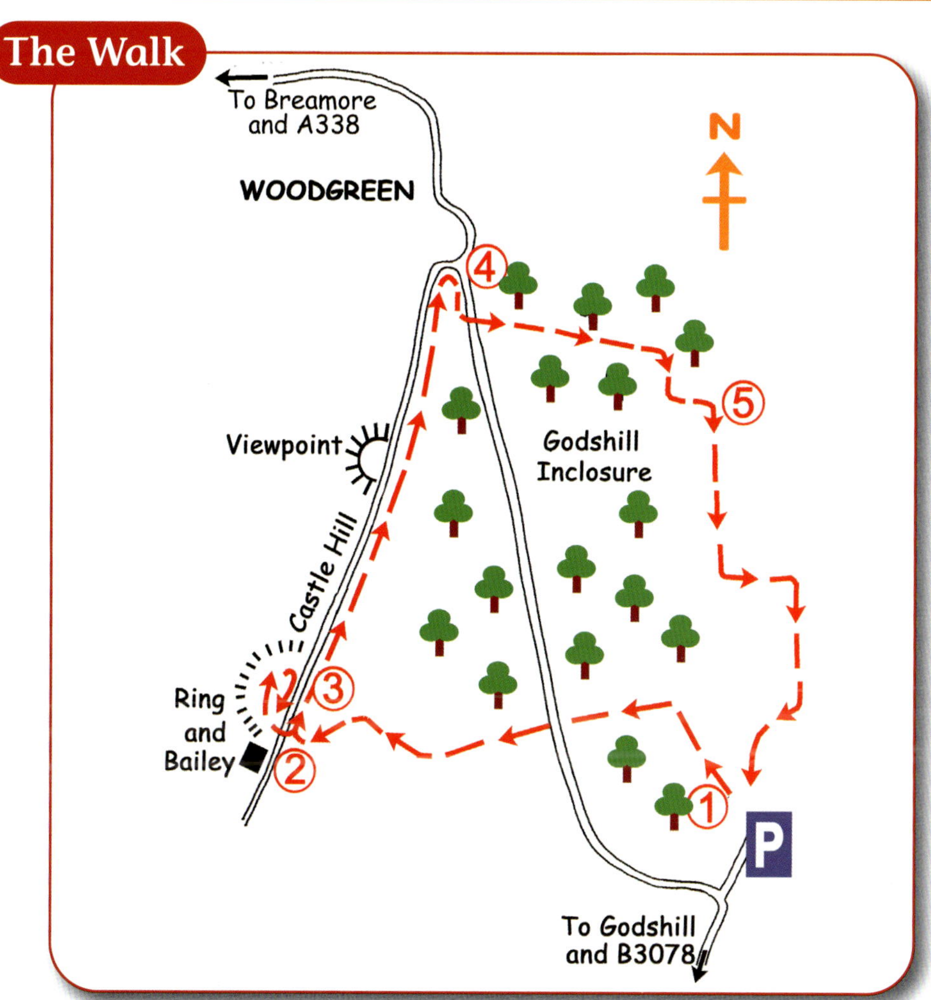

continue to the road. Cross the road, passing through the gates, and carry on through the woods. Fork right at a T-junction on the path and continue down the hill to pass through a wooden gate onto the road.

2 Straight ahead of you is the hill fort. To gain access to the fort, walk through wooden posts to the right of a house, climb up the hill and bear right past a house on the left.

4

An inquisitive pony in the New Forest.

3 To continue the walk, return to the road and carry on up the hill. After a while you will see a parking area and seats where you can sit and admire the lovely views across the valley overlooking the River Avon. When you are ready, continue along the road, which eventually drops down to a T-junction at Woodgreen village.

4 Turn right and then almost immediately cross the road to pass through a wooden gate on the left into Godshill Inclosure. Follow the path keeping straight ahead, ignoring the first two junctions of paths and at the third junction turn right then immediately left. This path takes you to a gate, which leads out of the woods.

5 Turn right and walk along the wide grassy path beside the wood. After a short while take a minor path on the left, which takes you to a gravel path. Turn right and follow the path, which runs along the edge of the hill. To the left there are lovely views across Millersford Bottom. Continue along this path to the car park.

◆ Background Notes ◆

Horses have roamed the New Forest since 1016 when local people were granted rights of common pasture, which allowed them to graze their animals in the forest. To improve the stock of the New Forest pony, other breeds were introduced, including Thoroughbred, Arab and Welsh and, in later years, this extended to British native ponies such as Dartmoor, Exmoor, Fell and Dale. New Forest ponies have gentle temperaments, are hardy and surefooted and are easy to train. However, for safety reasons, it is best not to let the children feed or stroke the ponies in the forest.

Most of the **ancient woodland** is deciduous, with the majority of trees being elm, oak and beech. Timber from the forest has been utilised for naval shipbuilding, including three of Nelson's ships used in the Battle of Trafalgar.

Nearby on the A338, the 17th-century picturesque village of **Breamore** has a Saxon church built in AD 980. Breamore House is an Elizabethan manor completed in 1583 and houses many articles of historical interest. The countryside museum has a collection of steam-powered farm machinery, historical tools and tractors, also a rare 16th-century Bavarian four-train turret clock, which strikes at quarter, half and hourly intervals. See how country folk lived in villages similar to Breamore, with replicas of a farm worker's cottage, dairy, wheelwright's, baker's, blacksmith's shop, brewery, village shop, cooperage, garage and a laundry. There is also an adventure playground! A short walk from Breamore House is a medieval turf mizmaze. This is thought to have been used by monks, who followed the circular path on their knees as a penance. Details from www.breamorehouse.com or telephone 01725 512468.

Testwood Lakes Nature Reserve

Water, water, everywhere

Reconstruction of a Bronze Age boat at Testwood Lakes Nature Reserve.

On the fringes of Totton and close to the M27, the 150-acre site of the Testwood Lakes Nature Reserve, which forms part of the Test Valley, is a pleasant oasis with an abundance of wildlife in its woodland, lakes and grassland. There is always much to see throughout the year – the woods are home to roe deer, foxes and birds, and from the hides and viewing screens you can watch many over-wintering wildfowl and waders on the lakes. There is plenty of history here too; archaeological excavations have revealed the remains of a bridge dated c1500 BC in Testwood Lake, and a piece of oak from a Bronze Age boat in Meadow Lake along with a Bronze rapier and spearhead.

Getting there *From the A36, turn into Brunel Road on the Calmore Industrial Estate. The entrance is 300 yards along on the left-hand side.*

Length of walk 1½ miles, or 2 miles if you include a walk to the hides.

Time Allow 1½ hours for the walk and perhaps add another ½ hour for a visit to the hides.

Terrain The paths are level and mostly on gravel; some are on wooden walkways.

Start/Parking The walk starts from the first car park, which is open from 8 am to 6 pm during summer, and 8 am to 4 pm in winter (GR 347154). Parking is free.

Map OS Outdoor Leisure 22 New Forest.

Refreshments There are plenty of benches along the route if you fancy taking a picnic. Tea, coffee and biscuits are also available at the visitor centre when it is open. The Vine Inn, Romsey Road, Ower (on the A36 north-west of the lakes) is a child-friendly pub with plenty of outside seating.

1 From the car park, go onto the gravel track and turn right. When you reach the lake, turn right and walk past a wooden gate and, when you reach a metal gate, bear left. Get the children to look out for short tree stumps with pictures of animals and insects carved

◆ Fun Things to See and Do ◆

The **two hides**, open from 10 am to 4 pm, are great fun to visit with plenty of information to help identify any birds spotted on the lake, including lapwing, heron and tufted duck. **At the pond** look out for kingfisher, emperor dragonfly, azure damselfly, marsh marigold, purple loosestrife, yellow flag iris, pond rushes and lesser spearwort.

At the **visitor centre** the children can see an exhibition of water, wildlife and conservation as well as interesting artefacts, including well-preserved timbers that still have the marks of carpenters' tools used in the Bronze Age.

5

The Walk

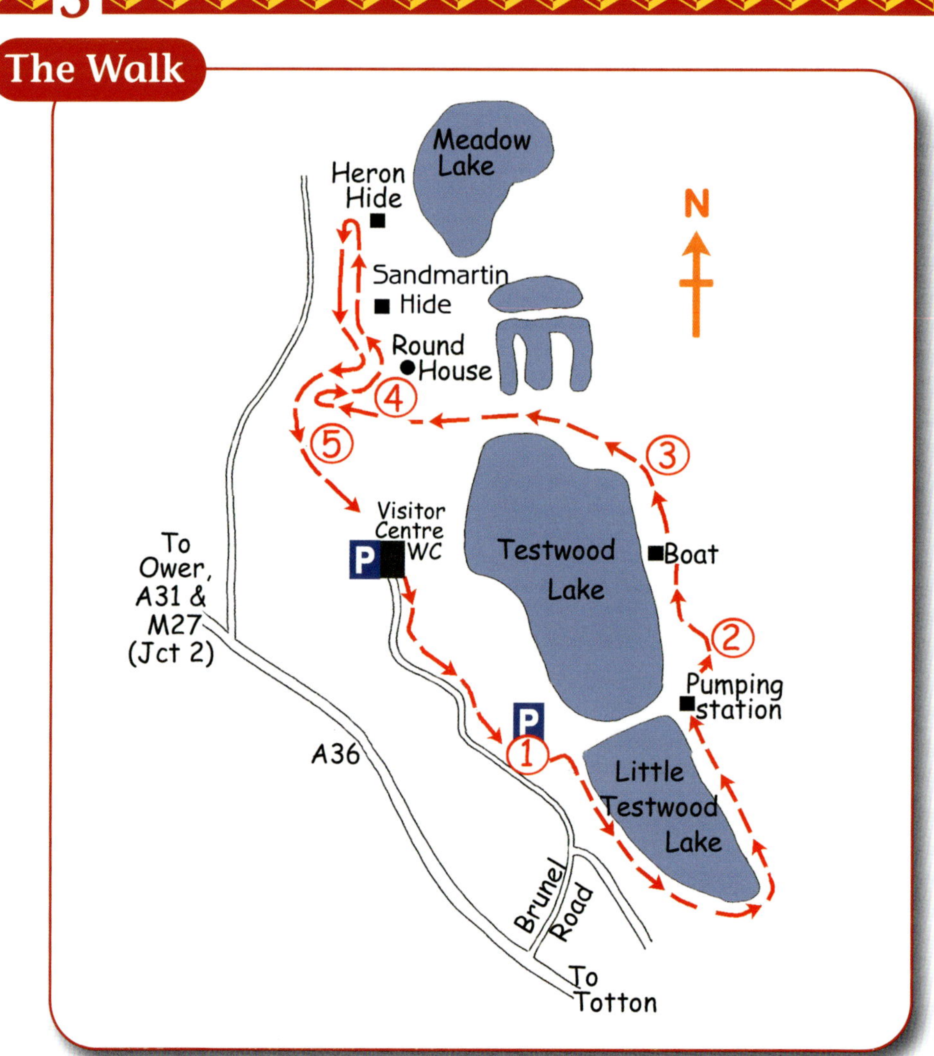

on the top. Go through a kissing gate and continue ahead to a pumping station, following the path around to the left, then pass through a kissing gate on the right.

2 Just before the next kissing gate turn left and, after a short while, leave the gravel track, aiming for the information board in front of the lake, where you will see the reconstruction of a

Bronze Age themed events are held at the Round House.

Bronze Age boat. Also get the children to look out for an interesting seat with sides shaped like a Bronze Age axe head.

3 Go back onto the gravel path and continue bearing left around to the next information board where the children can peer through the gaps in the wooden viewing screens to look for wildlife. Continue along the path and pass through a metal kissing gate. Carry on straight ahead, eventually following the path around to the right and pass through a small wooden gate into the children's education area.

4 Follow the gravel path to a pond and information board. Carry straight on through a wood along a wooden trackway, which leads to a field. Here you can see a reconstruction of a Bronze Age round house. Continue ahead along the wooden trackway and bear left onto a gravel path. The wooden screens allow visitors to reach the hides without disturbing the wildlife. Soon you will reach the Sandmartin hide.

Inside there is plenty of information about wildfowl and waders visiting the lake. Heron hide is just a short walk further along the path.

5 Retrace your steps back to the gate, follow the path around to the left and look out for a path on the right by a metal gate. This leads to the visitor centre. Outside the entrance is a small 'water wise' garden growing drought-tolerant plants. Follow the main track back to the car park.

◆ Background Notes ◆

Testwood Lakes is a relatively new nature reserve completed in 2002, which comprises of three lakes. Little Testwood Lake is a reservoir storing 270 million litres of water pumped from the River Test. Meadow Lake, which has two bird hides, is in a conservation area. Testwood Lake itself is a natural feature to encourage wildlife. For more information, visit www.southernwater.co.uk/homeAndLeisure/daysOut/testwood or telephone 023 8066 7929.

Very interesting **discoveries were made during excavations** carried out by Wessex Archaeology. At Testwood Lake they found 143 stakes, the remains of a 26 metre long construction, thought to be the earliest complete bridge found in Britain. A piece of oak 37cm long, discovered at Meadow Lake, is part of a cleat from the hull of a Bronze Age boat. Other finds include a single bronze spearhead and the blade of a short sword, known as a rapier, buried below the bridges at Meadow Lake.

The **round house**, which can be seen on the way to the hides, is used as an outdoor classroom at themed Bronze Age events. The walls are made of wattle and daub and the thatched roof is supported by 48 ash and alder rafters crossed with hazel lattice.

Manor Farm Country Park

Talking to the animals

Mum and her piglets at Manor Farm.

Manor Farm Country Park is situated along the banks of the River Hamble, halfway between Southampton and Portsmouth. Most of this short and pleasant walk takes you through ancient woodlands in the country park, which have been designated a Site of Special Scientific Interest. In spring you can see a wonderful display of bluebells and wood anemones. Some paths are not suitable for pushchairs, but there is a short circular walk along an easy access trail, which takes you down to the pontoon and viewpoint. After the walk you could then drive the short distance to Manor Farm and make it a whole day out. Most of the farm is accessible for pushchairs. For older children you could extend this walk by making a detour halfway around the route to visit the farm.

Kiddiwalks in Hampshire & the New Forest

6

Getting there *The entrance to the park is about ½ mile from junction 8 of the M27. Follow the brown signs for Manor Farm.*

Length of walk 2¼ miles but add another mile if you walk to the farm and back again.
Time Allow 2 hours for the walk but add extra time for a visit to Manor Farm.
Terrain This is an easy walk on level paths with a few steps to climb.

Start/Parking Park near the information point and toilets in Barnfield car park (GR 498111). There is a small charge for parking, which is refunded if you visit the farm.
Map OS Explorer 119 Meon Valley. Detail of all the tracks and footpaths in the park are on a notice board at the information point in Barnfield car park. Alternatively, you can buy the visitors' guide from Manor Farm reception.

◆ Fun Things to See and Do ◆

The highlight of this walk is the **pontoon on the River Hamble** where the children can watch boats as they glide past and look out for the many types of waterfowl that visit the river.

Manor Farm has all the right ingredients to keep the children amused. They'll love meeting the farm animals and visiting the Victorian school where they can marvel at the dunce's cap and teacher's cane. In the school playground they can have a go at simple Victorian games. There is also a play area in the picnic orchard, which has rare apple, plum and pear trees. Other attractions include farmyard walks, milking and an opportunity to meet the animals. You can also visit a blacksmith's forge, wheelwright's shop and a 13th-century church. Open daily from Easter to October and on Sundays and at half term for the rest of the year. For admission prices and opening times visit www3.hants.gov.uk/hampshire-countryside/ manorfarm or telephone 01489 787005.

The Walk

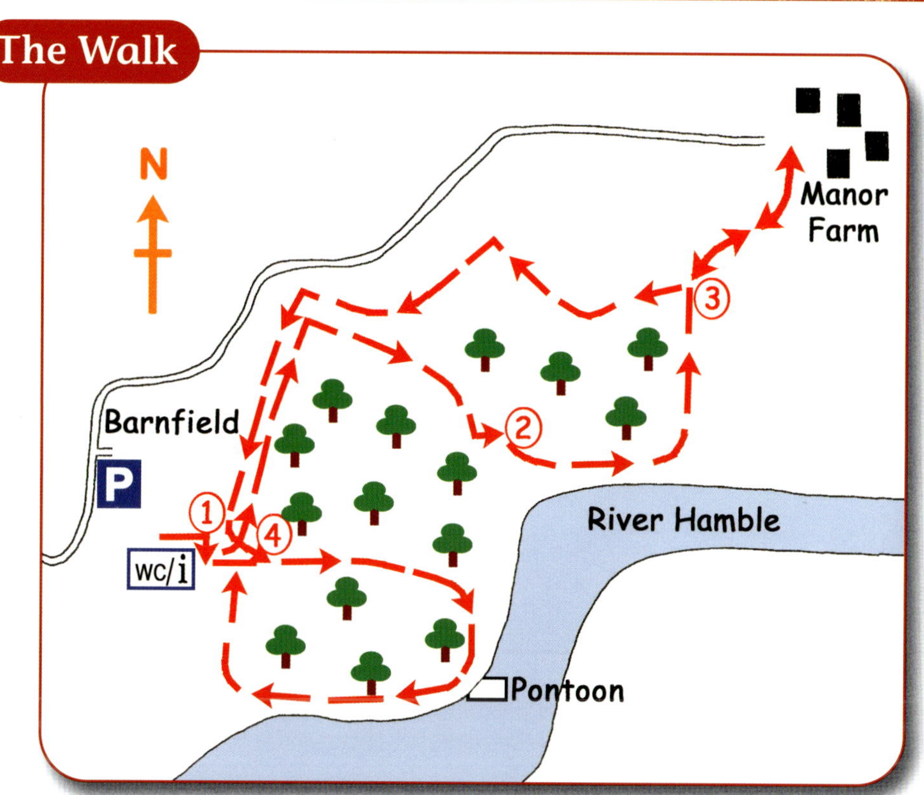

Refreshments There are two large picnic sites in the park, conveniently sited next to play areas. A kiosk at Barnfield sells ice-creams and soft drinks on Sundays during the summer months and also at bank holidays. Manor Farm café near the entrance to Manor Farm serves children's meals.

1 With your back to the information point and toilets, turn right and take the path running alongside the play area. Turn left at the sign for Manor Farm. When you reach the next signpost, turn right and follow the path round to a junction of paths then turn left onto the Strawberry Trail.

2 Cross a footbridge, climb some steps and pass through a gap in the fence. Ignore the left-hand path and continue ahead with the River Hamble on the right. After crossing a

When you visit the Victorian school, look for the dunce's cap.

footbridge take the left-hand path. When the path splits you can carry on ahead along the winding path for about another ½ mile to visit Manor Farm.

3 *To continue the walk,* take the left-hand fork and carry on to the next junction of paths. Turn right, walk through a gate and continue ahead between two fields. The hedges on either side are full of blackberries, rosehips and hawthorn berries in autumn. Take the next turning to the left by a log-seat (this section of path can be quite muddy in wet weather). Go through a gap beside a wooden gate and continue along the path until you reach a track. Turn left and follow the sign for the pontoon and toilets.

4 At the crossroad of paths turn left to follow a path to the pontoon. This is a pleasant spot for a breather where the children can look out for boats and hopefully see canoeists gliding past. Look for the yellow metal cross in the water which marks the final resting place of a medieval boat destroyed by fire after being struck by lightning. There is also a very interesting information board at this point. *To continue the walk*, follow the Strawberry Trail, signed to the Scout camp and activity centre. At the next fork turn right, continue to the next signpost and turn left to walk back to the car park.

◆ Background Notes ◆

The **Hamble**, meaning crooked river, is home to many birds including grey heron, black-headed gull, cormorant, little egret, curlew and redshank. Plants such as sea aster, marsh mallow, sea lavender, stiff saltmarsh grass and sea plantain can be found growing on the mudflats, which is an important source of food for birds and animals. The river was an important trade route for transporting bricks and timber to markets in the area but nowadays shipbuilding is the main industry in boatyards further downstream. In 1439 *Grace Dieu*, possibly the largest medieval naval vessel at 220 ft, was destroyed by fire after being struck by lightning and lies submerged south of the jetty.

Trees in the **ancient woodland** beside the river include oak, field maple, ash, wild cherry and crab apple. Look out for two rarer species, the wild service and small leaved lime. These woods were home to around 4,000 people in the 1940s in a secret Combined Operations Camp known as HMS Cricket. Following the decommissioning of the camp, many Southampton people lived temporarily in the buildings after losing their homes during the war.

Portchester Castle

A Roman adventure

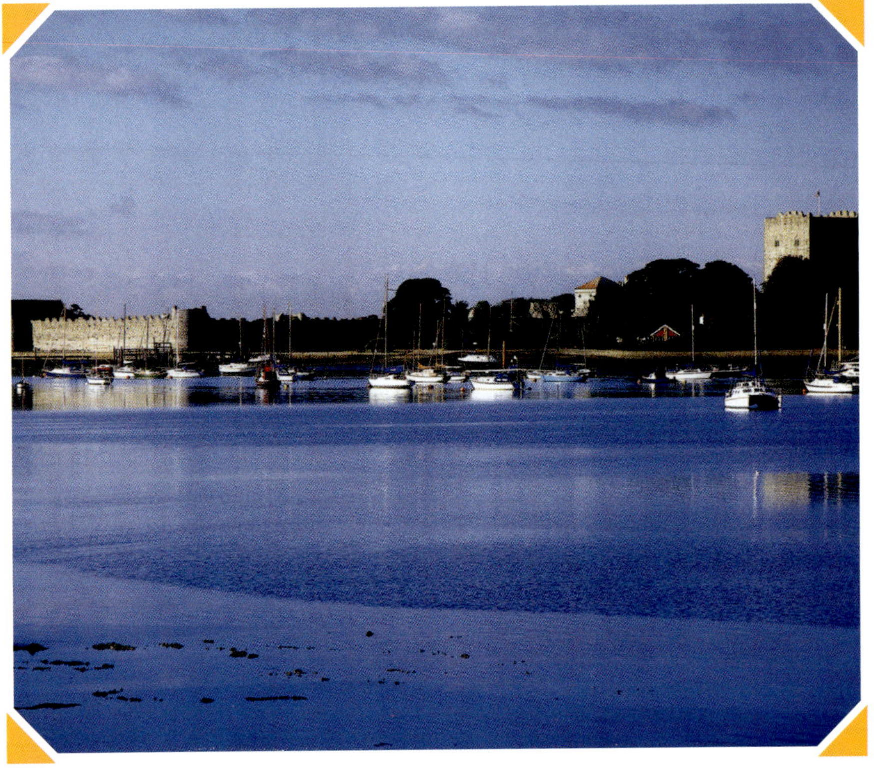

Looking across the harbour at Portchester Castle.

This is an easy family walk with something for everyone to enjoy and the entire route is pushchair friendly. Within the Roman walls of Portchester Castle is a large grass area ideal for a picnic. The children will love climbing the stone steps to the top of the Norman keep and from the top there are splendid views across Portsmouth Harbour. There is a play area in the recreation ground near the castle with plenty of space for ball games and part of the walk passes through Castle Shore Park, which is a good place to hunt for butterflies and wildflowers.

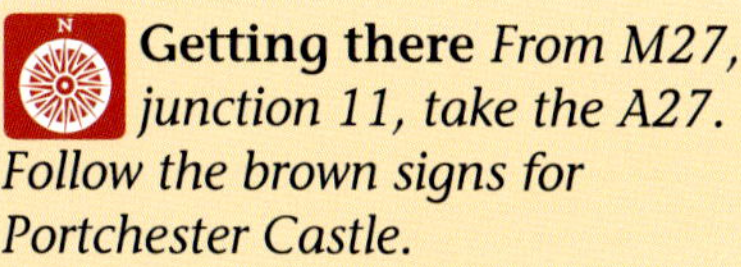 **Getting there** *From M27, junction 11, take the A27. Follow the brown signs for Portchester Castle.*

Length of walk 1 mile.

Time 1 hour but allow extra time for exploring the castle and a visit to the play area.

Terrain Paths are level, some on gravel, and all are accessible for pushchairs.

Start/Parking Start from the free car park, which has toilets, at Portchester Castle (GR 625047).

Map OS Explorer 119 Meon Valley.

Refreshments If you take your own picnic, you will find tables near the castle car park or you can sit on the grass inside the Roman walls. The shop in Portchester Castle sells hot and cold drinks and ice-creams. The Cormorant pub in Portchester has an outside seating area and a separate dining area inside for winter days. They also have a children's menu. Website: www.thecormorant.co.uk.

1 From the car park turn left and follow the path in front of the castle. Go past the toilets, and follow the gravel path around the perimeter walls of the castle. At this point you can enjoy the views and there is plenty of activity, with boats sailing to and from the harbour. A little further on note the holes high up in the wall, known as garderobe chutes, which were used in the 12th century as toilets in the Augustinian priory. Continue following the gravel path and head back to the car park.

2 By the picnic benches at the back of the car park you will see a small brick building. This is a

◆ Fun Things to See and Do ◆

In **Portchester Castle** you can climb to the top of the Norman keep for stunning views across the Solent, explore the remains of the palace and see many interesting artefacts found on the site. There is a charge for entering the keep but visiting the outer bailey and Roman walls is free. Details from www.english-heritage.org.uk or telephone 023 9237 8291.

The Walk

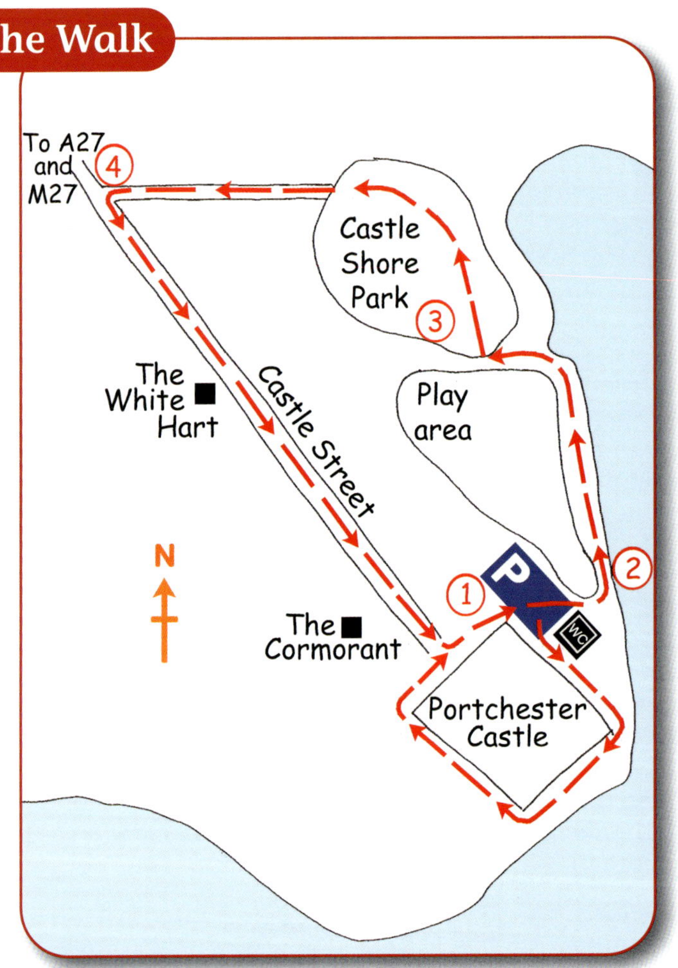

where you can see a play area on the far side.

3 At the end of the harbour wall, take the second path on the right, into Castle Shore Park. Continue straight ahead along the grass track through this lovely area, which is full of wildflowers and butterflies in the summer months. Take the left-hand fork when the path splits. Eventually you pass beside a gate and go onto a lane. Follow the lane to Castle Street.

4 Turn left into Castle Street to walk along the pavement past many attractive 18th-century houses and continue to the castle car park.

gunpowder store dating from around 1750 and was used by the military guard during wars in the 18th and 19th centuries. Walk along the path to the sea wall and bear left as it follows alongside the recreation ground,

◆ Background Notes ◆

Portchester Castle, sited on the edge of Portsmouth Harbour, was originally a Roman fort built to protect the coastline from Saxon invasion. The later addition of a Norman castle with a tower-keep in one corner was added in about 1090. King Richard II turned the castle into a palace in 1396. During the Dutch and Napoleonic wars the castle was used as a prison camp and until 1894 was a hospital and barracks.

In the 12th century a **priory** was built in the south-east corner of the outer bailey by Augustinian canons and consisted of sleeping quarters, storage buildings, kitchen, cloister and refectory. The monks later outgrew the priory and moved to Southwick, just north of Portsdown Hill. All that remains of the priory is **St Mary's chapel**, which is used as the parish church. In the churchyard look out for the recently restored grave and refurbished headstone of Thomas Goble who fought alongside Nelson at the Battle of Trafalgar.

Rising above the castle is **Portsdown Hill**, a Site of Special Scientific Interest with an abundance of wildlife on its chalk downland. Wildflowers to be found here are cowslips, coltsfoot, kidney vetch, yellow-wort, thyme, marjoram, common spotted orchid and autumn gentian. Birds include yellowhammer, skylark, whitethroat, blackcap, corn bunting and dunnock. There are many species of butterflies and moths including marbled white, meadow brown, orange tip, small blue and privet hawkmoth.

The **forts of Nelson**, **Wallington**, **Purbrook**, **Southwick**, **Widely and Farlington Redoubt** along Portsdown Hill top were constructed, at great expense, by orders from Palmerston's Government in 1859. They were built to defend the area against inland attack from French invaders but as no such attacks ever occurred the forts have since been known as 'Palmerston's folly'.

The magnificent **Nelson Monument**, sited on the top of Portsdown Hill, is only a short distance from Fort Nelson. It was designed by John Groves and completed in 1808. On top of the Portland stone obelisk is the bust of Lord Nelson.

Queen Elizabeth Country Park

A fun-packed day

Queen Elizabeth Country Park is the largest country park in Hampshire and is popular for walking, horse riding and cycling. Children of all ages will find something to keep them amused, with two separate play trails specially designed for different age groups. For families short of time, a quick walk from the visitor centre along an easy access path suitable for pushchairs will take you to the meadow, a grassy area ideal for picnics and barbecues. The Juniper Adventure trail is another quick option, which is also close to picnic areas and barbecue sites. For those wanting longer walks beyond the boundaries of the park there are several long-distance trails, including the South Downs Way, Hangers Way and the Staunton Way.

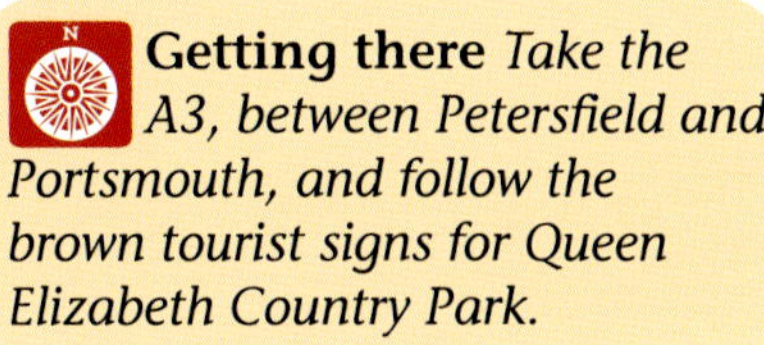

Getting there *Take the A3, between Petersfield and Portsmouth, and follow the brown tourist signs for Queen Elizabeth Country Park.*

Length of walk 2 miles.
Time About 1 hour but allow extra time for fun on the play trails.

Terrain Some gravel paths suitable for pushchairs; however, there are a few hills on this walk and bumpy tracks through the woods.
Start/Parking Start from the pay and display car park at the visitor centre (GR 718186).
Map OS Explorer 120 Chichester.
Refreshments There are plenty of picnic sites and barbecue areas

The Walk

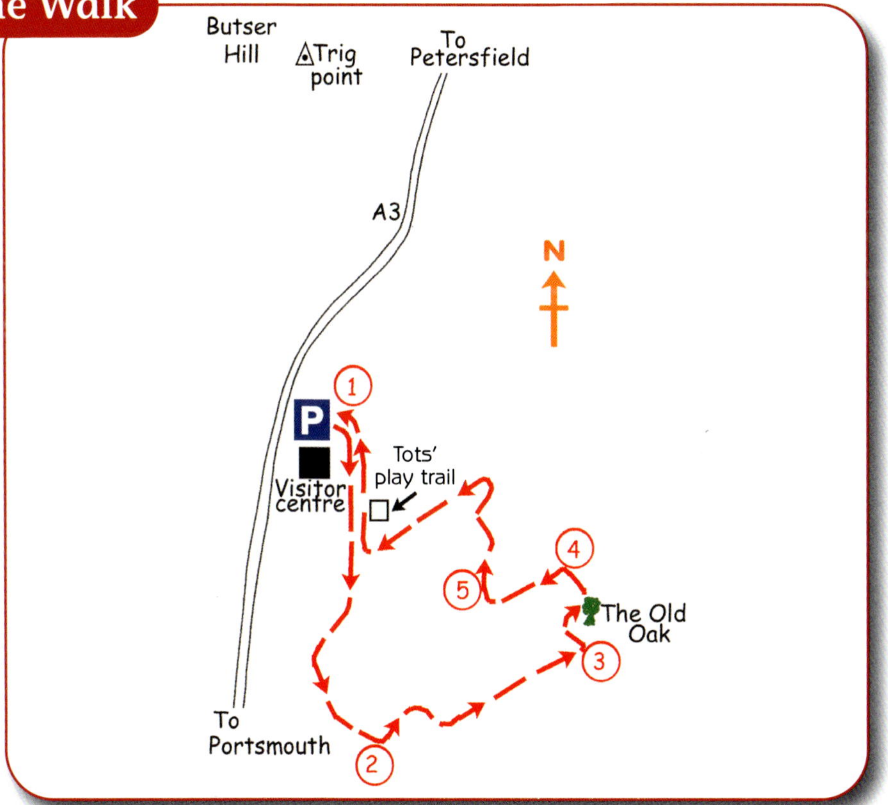

Kiddiwalks in Hampshire & the New Forest

within the park, and a café in the visitor centre serving Fair Trade tea, coffee and hot chocolate, as well as home-made meals and cakes. Seasonal kiosks can be found at the Juniper car park.

1 From the car park, either walk through the visitor centre and exit past the café, or take the path that goes around to the back of the visitor centre and café. Continue past the pond, tots' play trail and the meadow, which includes a barbecue and picnic site. When you reach the road, cross over and follow the red and green footprint markers onto the Staunton Way path. Continue up the hill – see if the children can spot the wooden posts with different planets carved into them. Take the right-hand fork when the path splits, still following the green and red markers.

2 At the next set of markers, turn left, following the red marker. Follow the twisting path uphill through the conifer wood. As you exit the wood, cross a main path and continue following the red markers into a deciduous wood.

◆ Fun Things to See and Do ◆

The **Juniper adventure trail** is suitable for children eight years old and above. The play trail includes a Burma bridge, rolling logs, rope swings and climbing nets and is sited near the car park, toilets and picnic area. For children aged two to seven years old, there is a **tots' play trail** near the visitor centre. The wooden play equipment includes a lizard wobbly pole, toad slide and grasshopper tunnel, all made by local sculptor Andy Frost. A map of the park and woodland fun sheets for children can be purchased from the visitor centre. For more information, visit www3.hants.gov/qecp or telephone 023 9259 5040.

Another short walk suitable for children is the downland trail of about 1¾ miles at nearby **Butser Hill**. This is also a popular area for kite flying, model gliding, hang-gliding and paragliding and there are special designated areas for these activities.

Toad slide in the Tots' Play Trail.

3 Look out for a wooden marker post on the left with '4X' on it and turn left onto a minor path. Follow the path as it twists and turns through the wood. Note the very old strangely shaped oak tree halfway up the hill.

4 At the gravel track turn left. Continue ahead, ignoring the first turning right. Take the second turning right onto a minor path with no waymarker sign, and carry on winding your way through a conifer wood. At the T-junction turn left and walk downhill with conifer trees to the left and beech trees to the right.

5 At the next T-junction turn right and continue to the road. Turn left, then almost immediately right to follow the path back past the meadow and tots' play trail and on to the visitor centre and car park.

◆ Background Notes ◆

Queen Elizabeth Country Park is sited within the East Hampshire Area of Outstanding Natural Beauty and is a mixture of chalk grassland, scattered scrub, ancient woodland, coniferous and beech plantations.

The highest point of the South Downs is **Butser Hill**, which lies partly within the park. The great majority of the hill is a Site of Special Scientific Interest and a Scheduled Ancient Monument with features such as lynchets, Bronze Age barrows, defensive earthworks, trackways and the site of a Roman farmstead. Designated a National Nature Reserve in 1998, the hill is also a Special Area of Conservation and is rich in wildlife with over 30 species of butterfly including the silver-spotted skipper, chalkhill blue and Duke of Burgundy fritillary. Flocks of Beulah and Manx sheep graze on Butser Hill, continuing the tradition of sheep farming on the South Downs. There are spectacular views from the top of the hill and on a clear day it is possible to see the Isle of Wight. To reach Butser Hill by car, you will need to return to the A3 and take the exit towards Hambledon/Clanfield/Chalton and turn left at Chalton Lane. At the roundabout, take the second exit. Turn left at Petersfield Road then the first right onto Hogs Lodge Lane. Take the first right and then turn right into Limekiln Lane which takes you to Butser Hill.

Butser Ancient Farm is an experimental, working Iron Age farmstead. The project was founded by Peter Reynolds in 1972 and originally the farm was at Little Butser on the site of an Iron Age farm on Butser Hill. It was relocated to Chalton in 1991 and can be found just off the A3 in Chalton Lane, not far from Queen Elizabeth Country Park. The farm is open on weekdays from Easter to September, between 10 am and 5 pm, but not at weekends unless a special event is taking place. For more information and admission prices, visit www.gallica.co.uk/butser2/farming or telephone 023 9259 8838.

Romsey

On the sculpture play trail

The Norman Romsey Abbey at the start of the walk is free to visit.

Romsey lies to the east of the River Test and is dominated by the Romanesque abbey, originally built in the 10th century. The walk first takes you past the abbey and then on to King John's House and Heritage Centre – best to allow a bit of extra time so that you can have a browse around this interesting museum (open all year round, Monday to Saturday). A stroll across the town then takes you to the nature reserve at Tadburn Meadows, which includes an unusual stone sculpture play trail.

Getting there *Romsey can be reached from the A3090 from Winchester or the A3057 from Stockbridge and Andover. It can also be accessed from either junction 2 or 3 of the M27. Head for the town centre then follow the signs for the medium stay car park in Newton Lane.*

Length of walk 3½ miles.
Time 2 hours but allow extra time for visits to the abbey, Heritage Centre and Tadburn Meadows sculpture play trail.
Terrain The entire walk is suitable for pushchairs along gravel footpaths or pavements. There are a few busy roads to cross.

Start/Parking The medium stay pay and display car park in Romsey town centre (GR 352 211).
Map OS Explorer 131 Romsey, Andover & Test Valley.
Refreshments Miss Moody's Tea Shop in the Tudor Cottage at King John's House.

1 From the car park head for Tee Court Arcade, which takes you through to the shops and town centre. Turn left at the road and continue to the Market Place. Turn left and pass through the abbey gateway. Shortly, turn right into The Abbey road and soon you will see the abbey on your right. After a visit to the abbey, exit from the main entrance and

The Walk

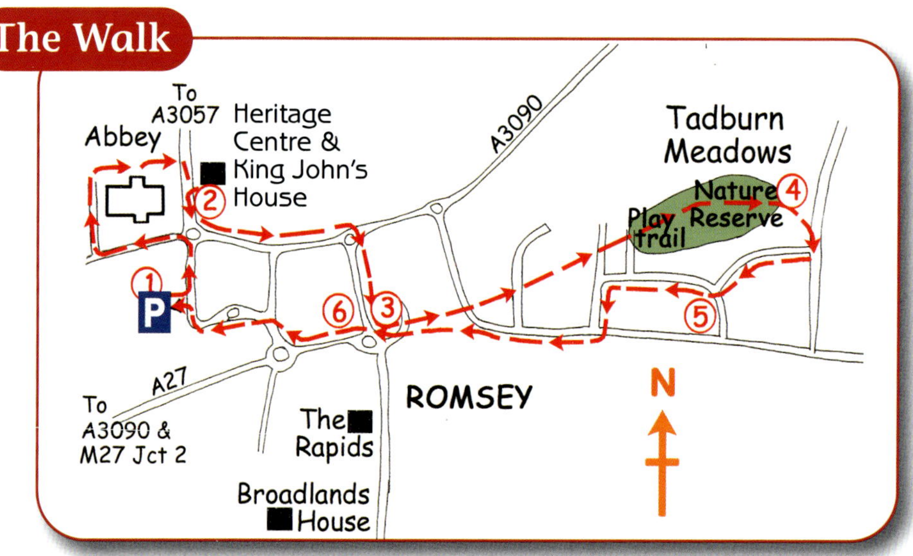

turn right. You will see the Heritage Centre and Tourist Information Centre straight ahead once you reach the road. You can obtain a free town guide and map from the Tourist Information Centre.

2 As you leave the centre turn left, and continue ahead to the Market Place. Keep to the left-hand pavement, which eventually takes you into the one-way system called The Hundred, and follow the signs for the Methodist church. Continue along this road past the Methodist church, following signs for Southampton Road and The Rapids. Carry on past the old brick and flint police station and cross the next road at the traffic lights. When you reach the roundabout, cross the road carefully and turn right, following the signs for Broadlands and the Rapids.

3 At the next roundabout turn left into Knatchbull Close and when you reach a lane cross over and take the path that runs between the allotments and a stream. Continue under the railway bridge and at the road turn right. Cross over at the crossing point then continue straight ahead onto a path beside a stream. Carry on to a road, cross over and continue ahead. When you reach the next road cross over; ignore the path

◆ Fun Things to See and Do ◆

Activities for children in **King John's House and Heritage Centre**, which is close to the abbey, include quiz trails, brass rubbings, picture colouring, mosaic pattern making and medieval gauntlets and helmets.

Tadburn Meadows Local Nature Reserve is 12 acres of open space with wet woodland, scrub, grazed meadows and a river running through the centre. Wildlife to look out for includes kingfishers, green woodpeckers and water voles. In the meadows is a **sculpture play trail** with a spider web climbing frame, stone bridge, human sundial, and pyramid steps with a slide.

straight ahead but bear left to take a path signed for Tadburn Meadows. At the next road, cross over and continue ahead with a stream to your right. Soon you will see Tadburn Meadows and the sculpture play trail. Follow the gravel path into the reserve.

4 Turn right over the second footbridge; keep on the gravel path and bear left, ignoring the steps going up into a housing estate. At the road turn right and after a short distance turn right again into Saxon Way. There is a convenience store halfway along Saxon Way where you can stop for an ice-cream.

5 At the T-junction turn right into Chambers Avenue. Continue ahead and at the next T-junction turn left into Hillside Avenue. Turn right when you reach the next T-junction, which is Botley Road. Continue past Hilliers Garden Centre and shortly after cross the road and turn left onto a footpath with a stream on the right. Retrace your steps under the railway bridge and past the allotments.

6 When you reach the roundabout cross over and bear left and carry on along the A27. At the next roundabout, which is by an entrance to Broadlands, cross over and turn right, heading for the town centre. Turn left into Broadwater Road, continue past Paimpol Place then turn right and cross over the road. Turn left and follow the road round into Middleton Street. Cross the road at the crossing, turn right then take a path on the left beside a restaurant, which takes you back to the car park.

◆ Background Notes ◆

King John's House and Heritage Centre is located within three buildings. **Tudor Cottage** is a timber-framed house, with period exhibitions from the 16th and 17th centuries in the upper room. **King John's House** includes medieval graffiti, roof timbers and a rare bone floor. **The Victorian museum** includes memorabilia from Victorian and Edwardian life in Romsey, Moody's gun shop, and a recreated parlour. For more information visit www.kingjohnshouse. org.uk or telephone 01794 512200.

West Meon

Down the line

The play area in Warnford village.

Part of this walk takes you along the old railway line, which is now a recreational trail and thriving wildlife corridor. It's hard to imagine as you walk along this peaceful path that steam trains rattled along the line between the embankments, carrying troops on their way to the docks during the First World War. In Warnford village, visit the playground for the children to have a go on the swings, slides and climbing frame. The walk then takes you across fields back to West Meon, where an ice-cream or home-made cake awaits you in the café behind the shop.

Getting there *From Winchester take the A272. Turn right at the traffic lights onto the A32, signed for Fareham. Approaching from the Alton direction, turn off the A31, onto the A32, just west of Chawton. When you reach West Meon, turn left into Station Road then turn right into a lane leading to Meon Valley railway line car park.*

Length of walk 3 miles.
Time 2 hours.
Terrain Most of the walk is along country lanes and across fields; there are three stiles. The A32 is crossed twice (see points 2 and 4).
Start/Parking Start from the West Meon railway line car park, which is free (GR 641237).
Map OS Explorer 119 Meon Valley.

Refreshments In West Meon Village there is a post office and well-stocked shop, which sells ice-creams. Behind the shop is a small, child friendly café serving all day breakfasts, light lunches and home-made cakes from 10 am.

1 From the back of the car park start the walk along the old railway line. Continue for about ¾ mile and when you see a bridge ahead, look for a path on the right, which takes you uphill to a road. At the road turn right and walk along Old Winchester Hill lane, which leads to the busy A32.

2 Cross the road with care and take the lane on the right-hand side of the George and Falcon pub. Walk to a T-junction in

◆ Fun Things to See and Do ◆

Wildlife you might see along the Meon Valley Trail are ringlet, orange tip, common blue and marbled white butterflies and birds such as buzzards, redwings and bullfinches. In spring you can see primroses, cowslips and sweet violets and during the summer months rosebay willow-herb and the common spotted orchid.

Older children would enjoy a visit to the ruins of **St John's House** in Warnford (see details in 'Background Notes').

The Walk

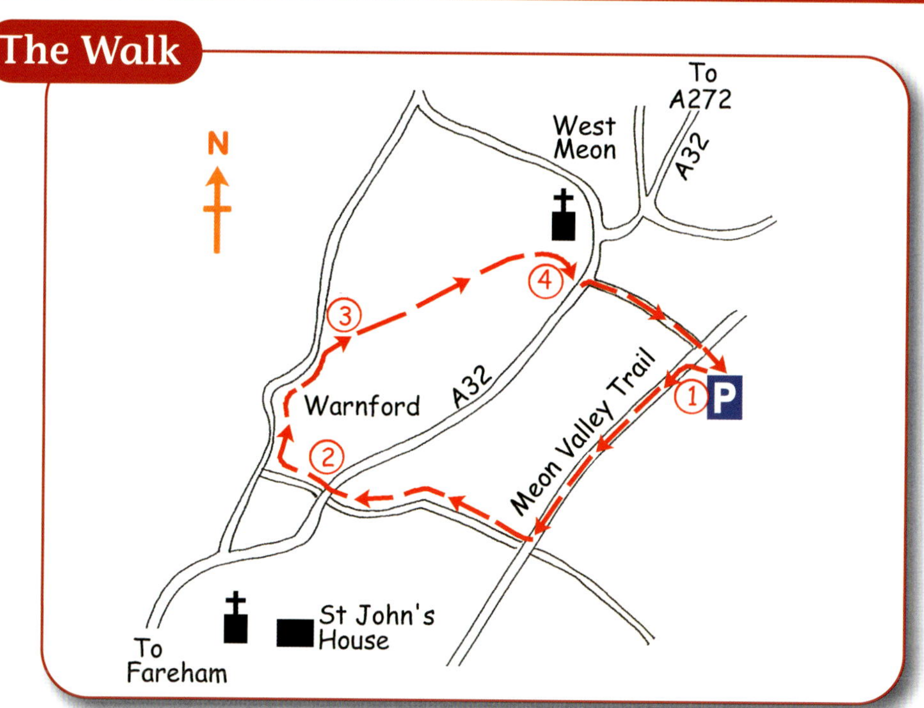

Warnford village and turn right. Very soon you will see the playground on the right with picnic tables near a stream.

3 As you leave the village, look for a stile on the right, which is opposite a farm entrance. Cross the stile onto a footpath and walk along the edge of the field, with views of fishing lakes across the valley on the right. Cross another stile and continue across the field where soon you can see West Meon village and church. Across the fields to the left is Lippen

Wood, the site of a Roman villa. Excavations in 1906 revealed the remains of a courtyard with mosaics, a hypocaust and a nearby bloomery (furnace for iron ore). When you reach a gravel track, follow the footpath, which runs between a flint wall and wooden fence. Cross a stone stile and walk across the churchyard to visit the parish church of St John the Evangelist.

4 When you leave the church, walk down the gravel path through the churchyard, go through a metal gate and follow the path down to the road. Turn left, cross the A32 with care and almost immediately turn right into Station Road. Continue back to the lane, on the right, which leads to Meon Valley railway line car park.

◆ Background Notes ◆

The **Meon Valley Railway** was a 22-mile line from Fareham to Alton, which took five years to build and was completed in 1903. It was busy in the early years transporting livestock to Fareham and Alton and delivering fresh produce, especially strawberries, to London. The line was withdrawn in August 1968 and the trackbed is now used as a recreational trail for walkers, cyclists and horse riders.

A visit to see the ruins of **St John's House**, a rare example of a 13th-century hall, is a must-see in February as the park and churchyard are carpeted with snowdrops. The house was built in 1210 by the St John family and is sited behind the church. The church of Our Lady was built in around 1190 by Adam de Port and stands in the privately owned park. The Norman tower is 50 ft high, built of Quarr stone from the Isle of Wight and contains six bells. An Elizabethan manor was built to replace St John's House, which was then utilised as a barn and finally became a scenic ruin after the estate was landscaped by Capability Brown in around 1760. The park is open every Sunday in February where you can park your car. To see the ruins at any other time of year, walk from Warnford village with caution along the very busy A32 for a short distance and into the park via a public footpath.

The **parish church of St John the Evangelist** is sited at the head of the picturesque village of West Meon. The church was built in the 1840s and is faced with square flints that were carefully knapped by the women of the village. It is said they were paid a farthing for each flint they knapped. In the churchyard is the tomb of Thomas Lord, the English cricketer who founded Lord's cricket ground. Also buried here are the parents of William Cobbett, author of Rural Rides.

St Catherine's Hill, Winchester

Be mizmazed!

Navigating the mizmaze on St Catherine's Hill.

This is a pretty walk that takes you alongside the River Itchen, past the historic buildings of St Cross Hospital and finishes at St Catherine's Hill. Although there is a steep climb up the hill, it really is worth the effort for the stunning views across Winchester City and the surrounding countryside. Of course, views don't really interest young children but one family I met on a cold winter's day were having a great time chasing their children around the paths of the mizmaze on top of the hill, and said this was one of their favourite destinations in Hampshire.

Getting there *From the M3, junction 9, take the A272. At the roundabout, take the second exit, signed 'Winchester'. At the next roundabout take the first exit, signed 'Bar End Industrial Estate'. At the third roundabout take the first exit, signed 'St Cross'. Continue along Garnier Road past St Catherine's Park and Ride, go under a bridge and you will see the car park on the left-hand side.*

Length of walk 3½ miles.
Time 2 hours.
Terrain Pavements and field paths; keep an eye on the children alongside the river as some paths are narrow. There is a steep climb up wooden steps to the top of St Catherine's Hill.
Start/Parking Start from the free car park in Garnier Road (GR 484280).
Map OS Explorer 132 Winchester, New Alresford & East Meon.
Refreshments St Catherine's Hill is a popular picnic area in the

◆ Fun Things to See and Do ◆

The bridge over the Itchen at point 3 is an ideal place to pause and **play pooh sticks**.

The fascinating **Hospital of St Cross**, which is open every day, is on the route of the walk (see point 2). Visitors can still receive the Wayfarer's Dole of a small beaker of beer and a piece of bread. For more information, see 'Background Notes'.

Children will love running in and out of the **mizmaze** on top of St Catherine's Hill.

In Winchester High Street is **Westgate Museum**, housed in a fortified medieval gateway that was a debtors' prison for 150 years. On display are weights and measures, armour, a gibbet and you can see walls covered in prisoners' graffiti. There are views of the city from the rooftop and children can take brass rubbings and complete a quiz. Admission is free. Telephone 01962 869864.

The Walk

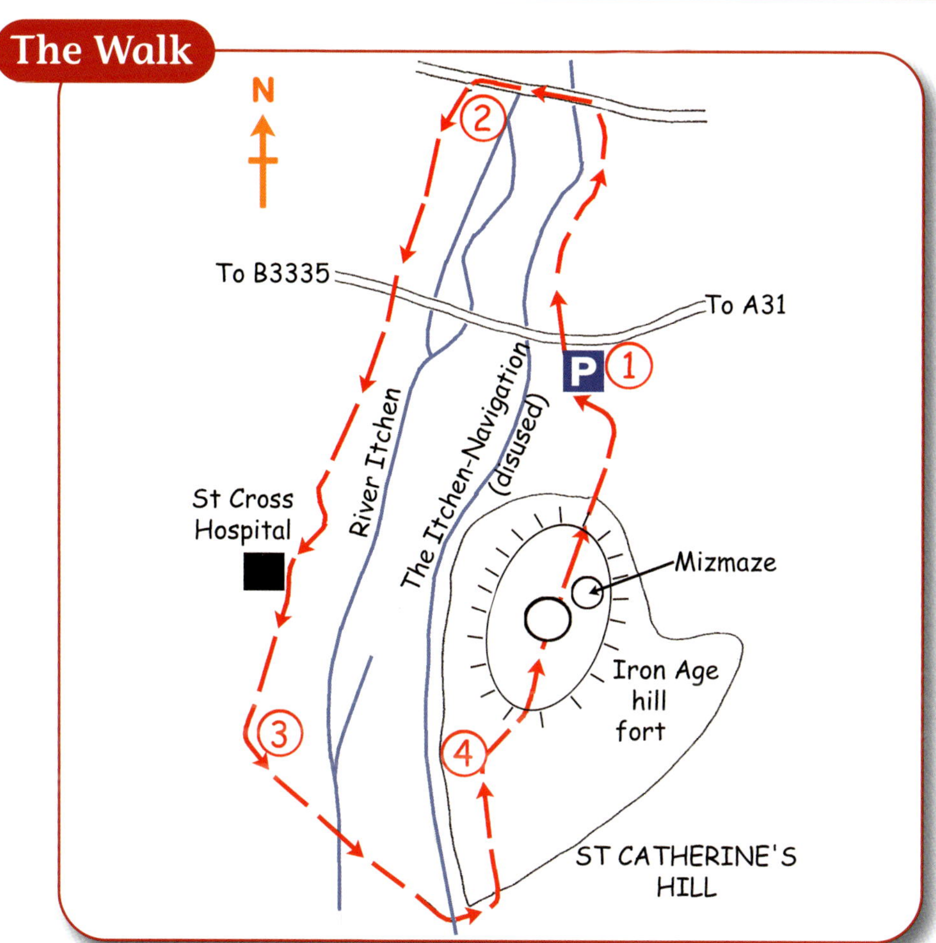

summer or you can picnic in the grounds of the St Cross Hospital. Tearooms in the Hospital open in the summer months from 1st April until 31st October, Monday to Saturday, 10.30 am to 12.30 pm and 2.30 pm to 4.30 pm. eighteen 71 at the Guildhall in Winchester High Street is family friendly, serves children's meals and has an indoor play area.

1 Walk to the road from the car park, cross the road with care, and take the footpath signed 'Pilgrims' Trail' straight ahead of you. Carry on along the path with the River Itchen on your left for about ½ mile. At a gate the path bears to the right, leading to a lane. Turn left and when you reach the road, turn left again. Walk across a bridge and continue ahead, following the sign for the water meadows.

2 Turn left onto a footpath with a stream on your right. After a short while you will be able to see St Catherine's Hill on the left. When you reach a road, cross with care and take the Clarendon Way path to the right of a brick and flint house. When you reach the end of the path, pass through a kissing gate and cross a footbridge. Ahead you will see St Cross Hospital, which can be visited by turning right at the footpath signed for St Cross. To continue the walk, carry on through an avenue of trees and cross a stile. Keep straight ahead with a stream on your right. Cross two more stiles, walk along a driveway and when you reach a road turn left.

The Hospital of St Cross dates from the 12th century.

3 Continue along this now disused road and cross a bridge that spans the River Itchen, which is a good place to play pooh sticks. To the right you can see a disused viaduct. At the end of the road, cross over the Itchen Way track and follow the path straight ahead, which leads up to the entrance of St Catherine's Hill. Climb up the hill, pass through a wooden gate, continue uphill and pass through a kissing gate. Follow the path through the trees then bear left down the hill. In the bottom of Plague Pit Valley are several rectangular burial mounds, the site of mass graves.

4 Climb up the wooden steps to the top of the hill where you can see Iron Age earthworks and are rewarded with stunning views. Continue across the top of the hill and walk through a copse of beech trees and out the other side where there is a mizmaze. Walk down the hill and follow a path, which takes you under a bridge and back to the car park.

◆ Background Notes ◆

Most of **St Catherine's Hill** is a Site of Special Scientific Interest and is part of East Hampshire's Area of Outstanding Natural Beauty. On the top of the hill can be seen the ramparts of an Iron Age fort, which is a scheduled ancient monument. In the centre of a copse of beech trees is the site of St Catherine's chapel, built in the 12th century, and close by is the mizmaze, which was cut sometime between 1647 and 1710. Shetland sheep graze on the hill throughout the year, keeping the grass short and creating an ideal habitat for chalk downland flowers including yellow rock-rose, horseshoe vetch, pyramidal orchid, greater knapweed, devil's bit scabious and autumn ladies' tresses. Twenty-five different species of butterfly breed on the hill including marbled white, brown argus and chalk hill blue butterflies, which can be seen during July and August. The hill is owned by Winchester College and is managed as a nature reserve by the Wildlife Trust.

Henry de Bliss founded the **Hospital of St Cross** between 1132 and 1136 to provide support for 13 poor men unable to work, and to feed 100 men at the gates each day. The Grade 1 listed buildings include a medieval hall and tower, Norman church, Tudor cloister and a peaceful Master's garden. There is an admission charge. Visit www.stcrosshospital.co.uk or telephone 01962 851375.

For details of the **Clarendon Way** see Walk 12, 'Background Notes'.

Farley Mount Country Park

Discovering a pyramid to 'Beware Chalk Pit'

Enjoying the view from Farley Mount.

The country park is an area of chalk down grassland and ancient woodland. West Wood, which is owned by the Forestry Commission, is a mixture of coniferous and broad-leaved woodland. Pitt Down and Beech Clump, which you pass through at the start and at the end of the walk, are rare habitats and the result of intensive sheep grazing. This has created ideal conditions for common blue and marbled white butterflies, five-spot burnet moths and plants such as salad burnet, sheep's fescue, bird's-foot trefoil, wild thyme and marjoram. At the end of the walk you can make a short climb up to the top of Farley Mount to see the monument to a beloved horse and admire the lovely views.

Getting there *From the B3049 turn into Woodman Lane, signed for Sparsholt. Drive through Sparsholt village and carry on for about 1 mile. Turn right at the crossroads, signed to King's Somborne, drive for about another mile then turn right at the junction. Continue for about ¾ mile and look for Juniper car park on the right.*

Length of walk 4 miles, which includes the walk to and from the monument.
Time About 3 hours.
Terrain Some paths are gravelled and suitable for pushchairs but be prepared for muddy areas in the woods in wet weather. There is a gentle climb up to the monument.
Start/Parking The Juniper free car park (GR 408293).
Map OS Explorer 132 Winchester, New Alresford & East Meon.
Refreshments Take a picnic to enjoy in Crab Wood or visit the child-friendly Plough Inn at Sparsholt village, which has a beer garden.

1 From the information board near the car park, take the path in front of you which runs to the right of the trees and follow the red marker posts – this is the Clarendon Way. Carry straight on

The Walk

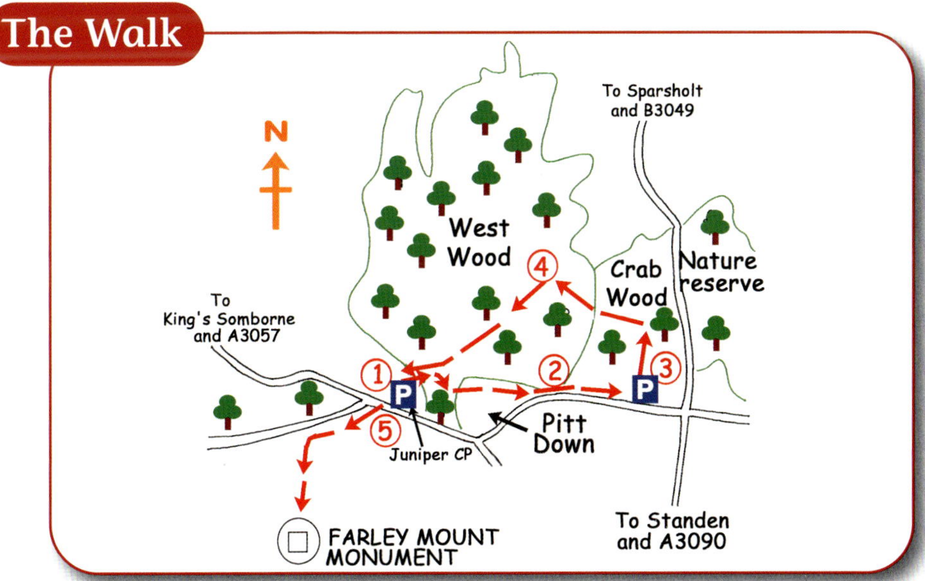

12

across a junction of paths and when you reach a gravel track turn right, then shortly turn left to continue on the Clarendon Way. Walk downhill through the wood, which leads out onto a grassy path. Keep straight ahead, following the red marker posts and ignoring tracks to the left and right. When the path splits, take the left-hand path.

2 When you reach the entrance to West Wood, ignore the bridleway sign and look for the narrow path that runs alongside the road, which continues as the Clarendon Way. Follow the path for about ½ mile until you reach Crab Wood car park. Turn left and walk across the grass area, which is a picnic site and play area, aiming for an information board.

3 Take the main path behind the information board, which leads into Crab Wood. Keep straight ahead, crossing a

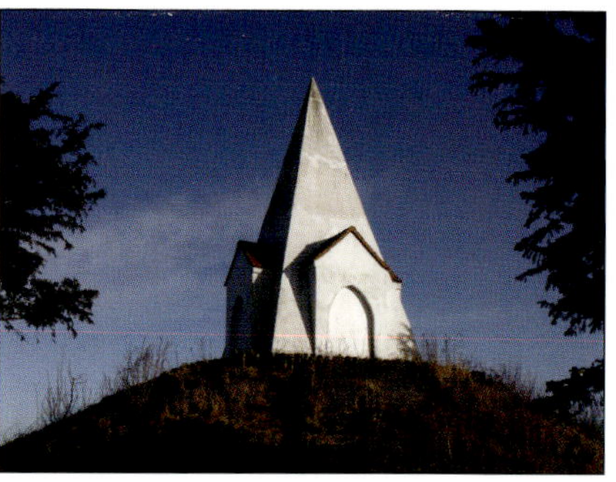

The Mount Farley horse monument.

junction of paths. At the next junction, turn left onto a path with red marker posts. When you reach a metal gate, cross over the gravel track and continue ahead, following a path through the wood.

4 When you reach a T-junction, turn left and carry straight on, ignoring paths leading off to the left and right. When you see the sign for West Wood, turn left and then almost immediately right to follow the grass path with the wood on your right. Keep following the path to a gravel track. Turn right and then left, following the signs for the

◆ Fun Things to See and Do ◆

Crab Wood is a popular area for **ball games** and picnics and on windy days Pitt Down is a good area for **flying kites**.

Clarendon Way, and pass through wooden posts. Continue through the woods, following the red marker posts back to Juniper car park.

5 If you want to see the monument, cross the road with caution, into the parking area opposite the entrance to Juniper car park. Walk straight ahead through the car park and continue on the gravel track at the other end. Climb up the hill and very shortly you will see the monument on the left-hand side.

◆ Background Notes ◆

Most of this walk takes you along the **Clarendon Way**, a 24-mile route starting from the River Itchen in Winchester and ending near the River Avon in Salisbury. The path is named after Clarendon Park, which is about 4 miles from Salisbury, and within the park lie the ruins of Clarendon Palace, a former royal hunting lodge.

Crab Wood is a Local Nature Reserve, which has been designated a Site of Special Scientific Interest and is an area of ancient semi-natural woodland covering 200 acres. The wood is managed using traditional techniques such as coppicing. The under-storey of mixed coppice is cut in different areas every 7 or 8 years and the resulting new growth is used for making thatching spars and wattle hurdles. This process allows maximum light to the ground, producing an abundance of woodland flowers, including a carpet of bluebells in the spring.

The unusual **pyramid-shaped monument** on top of Farley Mount was built in memory of a horse named 'Beware Chalk Pit', so called because he fell into a chalk pit 25 feet deep whilst out fox hunting in 1733. A year later his owner, Paulet St John, rode him to victory in a race on Worthy Downs. You can also enjoy stunning views of the Hampshire countryside from the monument.

For more information about **Farley Mount Country Park** visit www3.hantsgov.uk/hampshire-countryside/fmcp   or   telephone 01962 860948.

Danebury Hill Fort

A stroll back in time

If you fancy an easy stroll for an hour or so, then Danebury is just the ticket. Three really useful information boards will help the children understand how Iron Age people lived on the hill fort and there is, of course, the fun of climbing the ramparts whilst adults can admire the fantastic views across the Hampshire countryside. As you walk around today's peaceful setting, it's hard to imagine that 2,500 years ago there were 300 to 400 people living and working on the hill fort, which was surrounded by huge ramparts topped by palisades. From excavations carried out, there is evidence to suggest that these Iron Age people were a farming community keeping sheep and cattle, making leather goods and weaving woollen cloth.

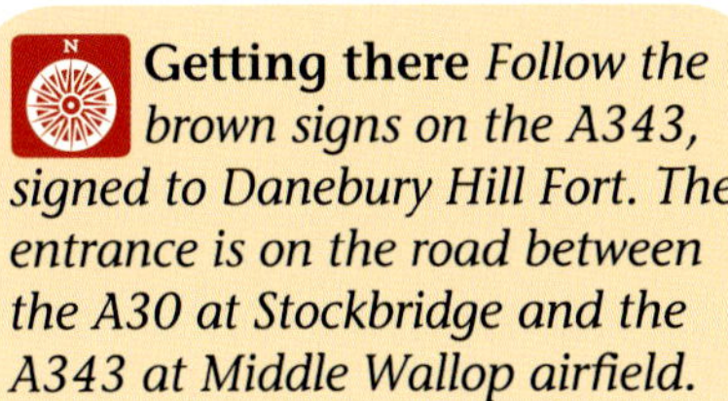

Getting there *Follow the brown signs on the A343, signed to Danebury Hill Fort. The entrance is on the road between the A30 at Stockbridge and the A343 at Middle Wallop airfield.*

Length of walk 1¾ miles.
Time Allow about 1½ hours.
Terrain There is a gentle slope up to the trig point. Once through the gates into the centre of the hill fort there are level paths suitable for pushchairs. The path around the perimeter of the fort is uneven in places with a few slopes and two kissing gates to negotiate.
Start/Parking There are two car parks. The walk starts from the second car park, which is next to the toilets. Parking is free (GR 329377).
Map OS Explorer 131 Romsey, Andover & Test Valley.
Refreshments I recommend taking a picnic for this walk. There are picnic tables in a field with lovely views; this can be reached from the car park by the toilets via some steps and through a wooden gate. If you visit the Museum of the Iron Age in Andover (see 'Background Notes') they have a small shop selling tea, coffee and biscuits.

1 From the car park, walk past the toilets and go through a wooden gate. A little further on is an information board that gives the history of the fort and the wildlife to look out for.

The Walk

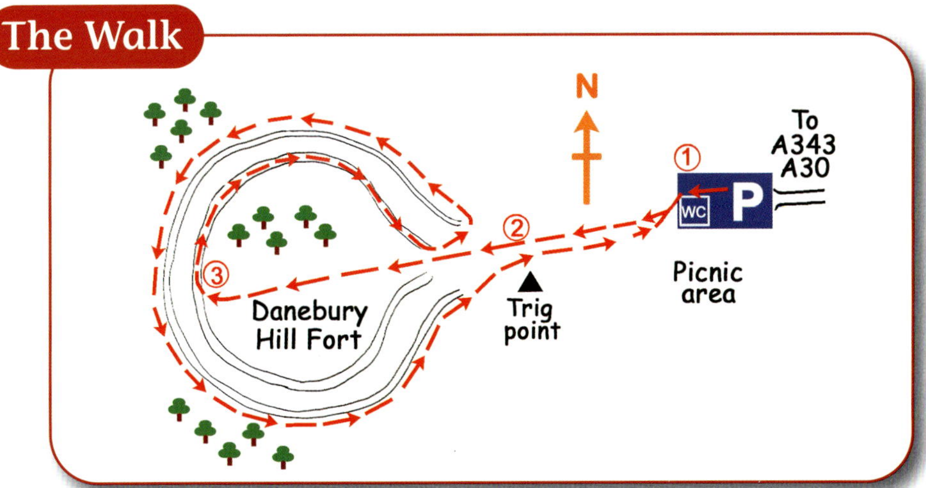

2 Walk past the trig point and shortly pass through two wooden gates. On the left is another information board; this one explains how the fort was constructed and has details of some of the excavations carried out. Continue along a gravel path, which turns into a grass path, leading to the final information board. This tells the story of how Iron Age people lived and worked at Danebury.

3 Continue ahead and climb up onto the rampart. Turn right and walk along the gravel path. There are fantastic views here and on a clear day you can see in the distance the huge white dish of Chilbolton Observatory, a facility for atmospheric and radio research which opened in 1967. Go down some wooden steps and back out of the fort through the two wooden gates. Turn left and follow a grass track with the fence to your left. After a short while pass through a kissing gate and carry on following the track around the outside of the fort to pass through another kissing gate. The path continues back to the trig point where you walk down the hill back to the car park.

These Manx Loghtan sheep graze on the Hill Fort.

◆ Fun Things to See and Do ◆

Children love **scrambling up and down the ramparts**. Get them to look out for a flock of **Manx Loghtan sheep**, originally bred on the Isle of Man, and the **Dexter cows**, which originated from Ireland. These are similar to hardy breeds that would have grazed here in the Iron Age.

◆ Background Notes ◆

Danebury is protected as a Scheduled Ancient Monument and is a Site of Special Scientific Interest. The **chalk downland is rich in wildlife** where you may see brown argus, marbled white and chalk hill blue butterflies and bloody-nosed beetles. Wildflowers found growing here include frog, pyramidal, common spotted and burnt tip orchids, horseshoe vetch, salad burnet and common rock-rose.

The hill fort affords fantastic views across **Danebury's Iron Age landscape** where you can see prehistoric burial mounds and several other hill forts. **Later additions to the landscape** include a 19th-century grandstand (south-east), provided for the Stockbridge races, the Chilbolton Observatory and Middle Wallop airfield.

Objects found during excavations, led by Professor Barry Cunliffe from 1969 to 1988, include iron and bronze artefacts, querns, bone combs and loom weights. A hoard of 11,000 sling stones found near the east gate indicates that they may have had to fight off attacks by raiding parties. Inside the hill fort look out for subtle dips in the ground, the site of deep grain pits. Grain was also kept in rectangular storage buildings. Round houses would have had thatched roofs with wattle and daub walls. In the centre of the ring the ground is raised with evidence of square buildings. These were home to the Druids, where religious gatherings would have taken place. To thank the gods for a successful harvest, there were ritual sacrifices of ravens, dogs, horses and sometimes even people, and they were thrown into disused grain pits.

The **Museum of the Iron Age**, in nearby Andover, has on display some of the finds discovered during excavations carried out at the hill fort. For an idea of life in the Iron Age, you can stand next to reconstructions of fortified ramparts and visit the roundhouse room, which is complete with a cooking cauldron.

For opening times see www3.hants.gov.uk/museum-of-the-ironage or telephone 0845 603 5635. Entry is free.

Alresford

Full steam ahead

Feeding the ducks on the River Alre.

A visit to Alresford is fun for all the family. A short stroll around the attractive Georgian town is suitable for pushchairs and includes a walk along the River Alre where ducks and fish are usually waiting to be fed. The return journey takes you through the recreation ground to the play area. This walk can be extended alongside the river to see the eel house. A visit to the station is a must, for a trip on a steam train through the beautiful Hampshire countryside.

Getting there *From the A31, take the B3047, which takes you into Alresford town centre. Follow the signs for the railway and car park.*

Length of walk 2½ miles or 1 mile for the short walk.
Time 1½ hours or ¾ hour for the short walk.
Terrain The short walk is on pavements and gravel paths suitable for pushchairs. The minor roads on the longer walk are quiet but they don't have pavements so keep a careful eye out for any traffic.

Start/Parking Start from Alresford station pay and display car park (GR 588325). Parking is free on Sundays and bank holidays.
Map OS Explorer 132 Winchester, New Alresford & East Meon.
Refreshments The war memorial garden (see point 2) would be ideal for a picnic. The Tiffin Tea Rooms in West Street has outside seating in a courtyard to the rear and serves light lunches and home-made cakes. The Cricketers Inn in Jacklyns Lane is a family friendly pub with a large outdoor play area.

The Walk

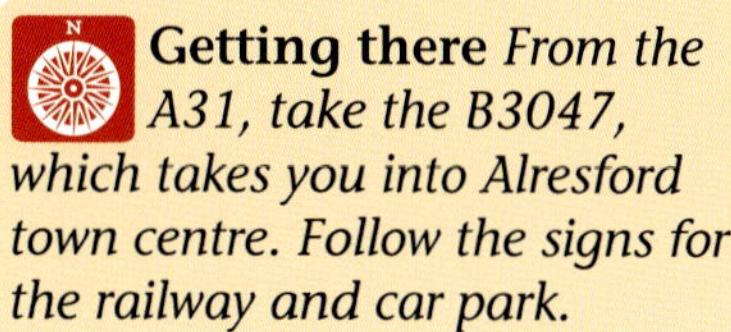

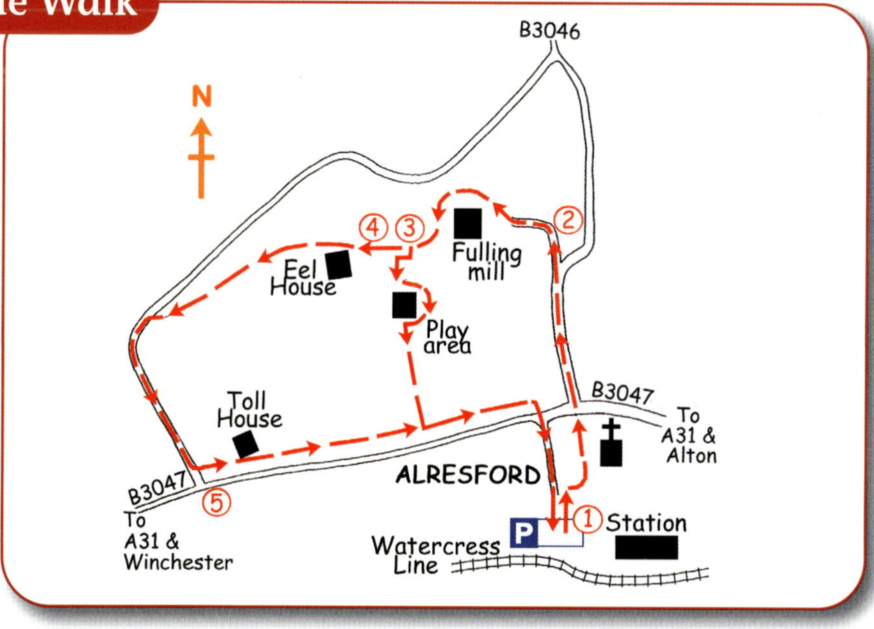

1 From the car park, walk back down Station Road and turn right, opposite the toilets, onto a footpath leading to the churchyard then turn left to walk past the church of St John the Baptist. Just before the road there is an information board. Cross the road with care and continue straight ahead along Broad Street, which has many fine Georgian houses and interesting shops. There is an information board halfway down the street.

2 Walk down Mill Hill to another information board on the right. Turn left into Ladywell Lane, which leads to a gravel path. You are now on the Wayfarer's Walk, a 70 mile route between Emsworth on the coast near Portsmouth to Inkpen Beacon in Berkshire. Soon you will see on the left the war memorial garden, which is a good spot for a picnic. Continue alongside the River Alre to the thatched fulling mill, which was built in the 13th century. Along this stretch of the river there are usually ducks to feed and watercress can be seen growing on the opposite side of the river just past the mill. When you reach the road turn right to follow the footpath with the river on your right. After a short while you will see an information board by a kissing gate.

◆ Fun Things to See and Do ◆

In 1997 part of the River Alre was designated a Site of Special Scientific Interest and there is **plenty of wildlife** to be seen. It is home to less common animals and birds including water voles, otters and water rails. You might also glimpse kingfishers, herons, little egrets and brown trout. Wildflowers include ragged robin, meadowsweet and flag iris.

The **Watercress Line** at Alresford is well worth a visit – there is a lot to see at the station, and even more on one of its special activity days. For details of the line, visit www.watercressonline.co.uk or telephone 01962 733810.

Steam train on the watercress line, Alresford.

❸ At this point, *if you are following the shorter walk,* pass through the kissing gate into the recreation ground. Follow the gravel path to the right, which passes a skateboard park and a little further on is the play area. Continue along the gravel path to the road, turn left and walk into the town. Turn right into Station Road to return to the car park.

❹ *To continue the main walk,* carry on beside the river and soon you will see a small brick building called the eel house. This was built in the 1820s and the three brick-lined channels underneath would have contained eel traps. Walk to the right of the eel house and follow the path, which eventually passes houses on the left and skirts a private parking area. Continue ahead along the footpath, which shortly merges into a lane. Follow the lane as it bears left and walk for ¼ mile to Winchester Road.

5 Turn left and head back towards the town along The Avenue, a pleasant walk between mature lime trees. This was originally a recreation area owned by the Bishop of Winchester. Look out for Turnpike House, a red-brick hexagonal building on the left, which used to be a toll house. It was built this unusual shape to allow the keeper an all-round view and prevent anyone trying to avoid paying the toll. Walk into the town along Pound Hill. Cross the road and carry on along West Street. Turn right into Station Road to return to the car park.

◆ Background Notes ◆

The **fulling mill** is now a private house but in the 13th century it contained water-driven hammers called fuller stocks which beat raw cloth into usable material.

The **eel house** dates from the 1820s and was probably used to catch eels in traps which would have been under the building in three brick-lined channels. Nowadays these channels control the river flow.

There have been a number of **destructive fires** in the town of Alresford; the first was in 1440 and this was followed by another in 1689 where the church, market house and 117 houses were destroyed. After the last fire in 1736, the town was rebuilt in the Georgian style, which can be seen in the elegant houses along Broad Street.

Watercress has been commercially grown in Alresford since the 1860s. Clean, pure water from fast flowing springs in the area provide ideal growing conditions for the plants and the constant temperature of the water allows year round cultivation.

The **Watercress Line** runs ten miles between Alresford and Alton, gaining its popular name from the 1860s when the locally grown watercress was transported by train to London.

Alton

A playtime delight

The Gallery of Childhood in Alton.

There is plenty to see and do on this walk around the market town of Alton. First is a visit (Tuesday to Saturday) to the Curtis Museum in the High Street for a wander around the Gallery of Childhood, then a short walk takes you to St Lawrence church where you can show the children bullet holes in the inner doors which occurred during the Civil War. In Paper Mill Lane is Alton station – the terminus for the Watercress Line, a restored heritage steam railway. Next is a leisurely stroll around King's Pond where there is an abundance of wildlife to see. At one time there was a mill by the pond, which manufactured paper. On the return journey, as you walk along Lower Turk Street, you'll probably smell that distinctive aroma of hops brewing when you pass Coors Brewing Company, which produces Worthington, Grolsch and Carling. Brewing has been one of the main industries in Alton since 1763, with hops and barley grown in the surrounding area. If the children are still raring to go at the end of the walk, there is a play area in the Public Gardens.

15

Getting there *From the A31 take the A339. At Alton, follow the brown signs to the town centre and museums and then follow the signs to Lady Place car park.*

Length of walk 2 miles.
Time About 1½ hours. Allow extra time for a visit to the museum.
Terrain The entire walk is along pavements and suitable for pushchairs. Take extra care when crossing the busy roads.
Start/Parking The walk starts from Lady Place pay and display car park in Alton (GR 715393).

Map OS Explorer 144 Basingstoke, Alton & Whitchurch.
Refreshments If you take a picnic, there are seats and benches in the Public Gardens and also seats around King's Pond. Alternatively, you will find the English Garden Restaurant in Normandy Street.

1 From Lady Place car park head for the Public Gardens and toilets. Follow the tourist signs to the market square and town centre. In the market square head for Westbrook Walk, which takes you through a shopping arcade,

The Walk

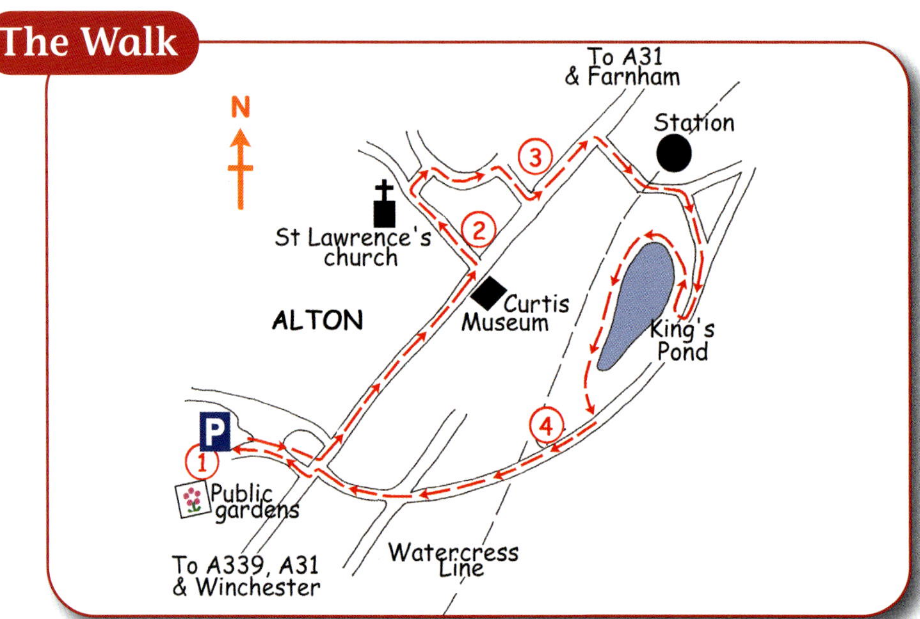

past a large statue of a brown bear and onto the High Street. Turn left and walk up the road to the Curtis Museum, which is on the right just before the mini roundabout. Note the Cairn war memorial alongside the museum, often referred to as 'a pile of stones'.

2 After a look around the museum, cross the road and turn left into Church Street for a visit to St Lawrence church. To continue the walk, turn right into Chauntsingers Road, which bears around to the right. Take the first right turn, after the entrance to a car park, into Victoria Road.

3 At the end of the road turn left. After walking past a mini roundabout, cross the road at the traffic lights and shortly turn right into Paper Mill Lane. Follow this road past the turning for the station and continue under a bridge then up the hill and turn right into Ashdell Road. After a short distance you will see a path on the right leading to King's Pond, which has an interesting information board. Walk straight ahead and follow the path, with the pond to your left. Eventually the path leads to a road.

4 Turn right and walk under the bridge, continuing along Lower

◆ Fun Things to See and Do ◆

Children will enjoy a wander around the **Curtis Museum** in the High Street, to see the **Gallery of Childhood**. Jigsaws, toys and books are displayed in low cases, an ideal height for youngsters, and there are two furnished dolls' houses.

The **church of St Lawrence** is worth a visit. At the end of the Civil War, during the Battle of Alton in 1643, Royalist soldiers took refuge from Parliamentary troops in the church. You can still see round bullet holes, and also rectangular openings, which allowed guns to be fired through, in the inner doors.

King's Pond is a wonderful spot for **bird-watching**, and in spring and summer there are lots of **wildflowers to identify** (see 'Background Notes').

Turk Street to the mini roundabout at Drayman's Way. Cross the road and walk straight ahead into Turk Street. This leads back to the High Street. Turn left and then cross the road to walk back through Westbrook Walk. Continue through the market square to Lady Place car park.

Many birds can be seen at King's Pond, Alton.

◆ Background Notes ◆

The **Curtis Museum** was named after Dr William Curtis, a botanist who was born in Alton. As well as the Gallery of Childhood there are local history exhibitions and artefacts including the highly decorated Roman 'Selbourne Cup' and the 'Alton Buckle', which was found in the grave of an Anglo-Saxon warrior. Entry to the museum is free. For more information and opening times visit www.hants.gov.uk/museum/curtis or telephone 0845 603 5635.

King's Pond was named after Mr William King, a local paper maker. The River Wey was dammed in the 18th century to form the pond, providing headwater for the nearby paper mill. Resident birds you can see on the pond are moorhens, coots, tufted ducks, mute swans and mallards. In summer the pond is visited by swifts and house martins. Other birds to look out for are kingfishers, herons, grey wagtails, Canada geese, song thrushes and chaffinches. The grassy areas alongside the pond are covered in wildflowers in spring and summer including cowslips, ox-eye daisies, yarrow, black knapweed and musk mallow. Along the banks you can see great willow-herb, yellow flag and hemp agrimony. Some of the trees growing around the pond are alder, sycamore, willow and horse chestnut.

For details of the **Watercress Line** with its steam trains running between Alresford and Alton, see Walk 14.

Whitchurch

Feed the ducks!

A resident at the River Test, Whitchurch.

Whitchurch is an attractive town with many listed buildings within a conservation area, and the River Test, which is a Site of Special Scientific Interest, flowing through it. To the north and west of the town are the North Wessex Downs, an Area of Outstanding Natural Beauty. The highlight of the walk for the children will probably be feeding the ducks in the pond by the Silk Mill and alongside the river as you walk to the Fulling Mill. Oats, corn, chopped lettuce or defrosted frozen peas are better for ducks than bread. The Millennium Meadow, a green 'breathing space' for the community is a great place for ball games and a picnic.

16

Getting there *From the A303 east of Andover, take the B3048 northwards. Continue through Longparish and turn right at the T-junction in Hurstbourne Priors. Follow the B3400 to Whitchurch.*

Length of walk 1½ miles.
Time About ½ hour, but allow extra time to spend in the meadow and feeding the ducks.
Terrain All paths are level.
Start/Parking Park in the Whitchurch Silk Mill car park, which is free (GR 463478).
Map OS Explorer 144 Basingstoke, Alton & Whitchurch.
Refreshments There are picnic tables and seats in the Millennium Meadow. The Village Bakery in Bell Street sells hot drinks, snacks and sandwiches. Alternatively, children are welcome at The Kings Arms in Whitchurch.

1 From the Silk Mill car park, turn left into Winchester Street. You can feed the ducks in the mill pond by the bridge but save some food as there might be more ducks to feed later in the walk. Continue to a roundabout and turn left into Church Street. Cross the road and continue on the pavement to All Hallows church. Among some of the interesting things to see in the church are a Tudor font and the 'Saxon stone' found during renovations by the Victorians and believed to be from the original Saxon church.

2 Look out for a footpath sign opposite the church as the road bends to the right. Cross the road with caution and take the footpath, which leads you to the river.

3 Turn right and follow the path alongside the river – keep an eye on the children as the way is

◆ Fun Things to See and Do ◆

In **Whitchurch Silk Mill** you can watch an introductory video explaining the history of making silk, see Victorian weaving machinery and perhaps have a go at weaving on a handloom. During the week there are skilled weavers at work. Outside there is a working water wheel as well as the duck pond.

The Walk

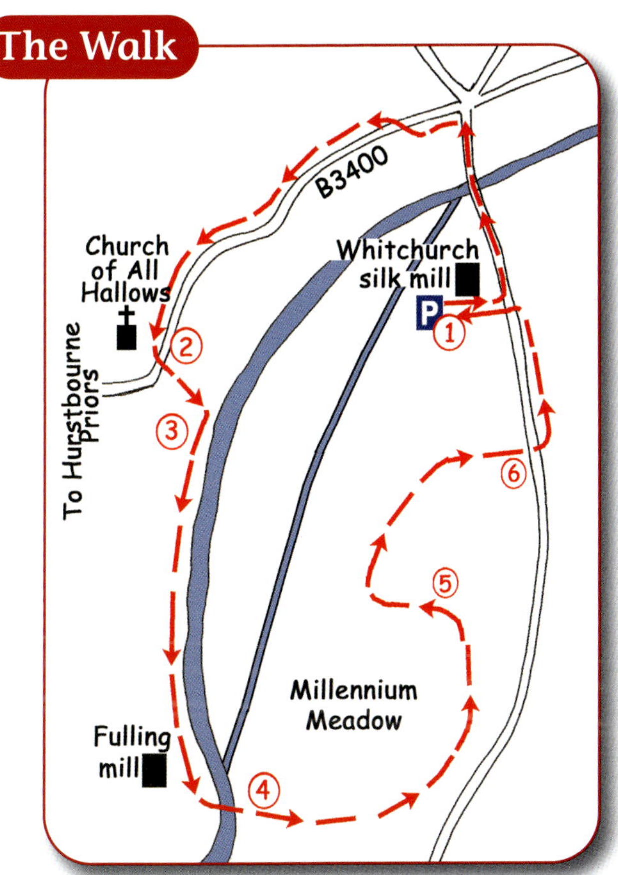

4 This path takes you over a footbridge and into the Millennium Meadow, which is managed as a wildlife environment. The clear water of the stream is achieved by narrowing the banks, enabling the water to flow faster, which in turn helps to keep the bottom of the stream clean.

5 Bear left around the meadow and at various points the children can have fun searching for small wooden posts with colourful pictures and information about the wildlife. Look out for a small pond where you might see dragonflies and damselflies in the summer months.

6 To continue the walk, go through the iron gates at the far end of the meadow and turn left into Winchester Street. Cross the road and walk along the pavement back to the Silk Mill car park.

quite narrow. There are usually ducks along this stretch of the river to feed and wildlife to watch out for includes coot, moorhen, heron, kingfisher and trout. Eventually you reach a footbridge at the Fulling Mill. Cross the footbridge and at the entrance to the mill bear slightly left and take the footpath on the opposite side of the road.

16

◆ Background Notes ◆

During the 18th and 19th centuries **Whitchurch mills** manufactured flour, woollen cloth and silk, and nearby Bere Mill, owned by Henry Portal, produced high-quality paper which was supplied to the Bank of England.

Whitchurch Silk Mill was built in 1800 on the River Test, and specialises in producing silks for interior designers, historic houses and costume dramas. It is open all year round from Tuesday to Sunday and on Bank Holiday Mondays. Details from www.whitchurchsilkmill.org.uk or telephone 01256 892065.

The parish **church of All Hallows** was built in the 12th century, but most of the original Norman structure was removed by the Victorians when they extended the church in the middle of the 19th century. However, before the Normans arrived, there was a small white church, which was either constructed from chalk blocks or the building was whitewashed, hence the town's name of Whitchurch.

A picturesque part of the walk is by the **Fulling Mill** (now a private house), where the clear water of the River Test is renowned as being one of the finest trout rivers in England. The fulling process involves cleaning cloth to remove dirt and oil and then thickening the cloth using water, which mats the fibres together. During the medieval period, water mills were used in the process – the cloth was beaten with wooden hammers driven by machinery, which was powered by the water wheel. In the Roman period, slaves would tread the cloth with bare feet in tubs of human urine; ammonium salts in the urine helped to clean the cloth!

The most **famous residents** of Whitchurch include the late Lord Denning, one of the most influential judges of the 20th century who was born above a draper's shop in the town, and Richard Adams, the author of *Watership Down*.

Basingstoke Common

A Civil War saunter

A re-enactment of the English Civil War at Basing House.

If your children fancy a short stroll and a play on the swings, then Basingstoke Common is the place to visit. The play area is well equipped, with the bonus of a picnic site and barbecue area all within close range of the car park. For older children the longer walk takes you across the common, through old Basing village, past a Tithe Barn and then a short walk to the ruins of Basing House, which are open in the summer months and are well worth a visit.

17

Getting there *Leave the M3 at junction 6 and take the A30 towards Hook. Turn first left after the roundabout into Redbridge Lane, then turn right into Basing Lime Pits car park.*

Length of walk 3¼ miles if you visit Basing House; 1½ miles for the shorter walk.

Time The short walk takes about ¾ hour. Allow 2 hours for the longer walk.

Terrain Mostly field paths and minor roads. There are a few steep steps to climb at the start of the walk.

Start/Parking Park in Lime Pits car park, which is free (GR 654522).

Map OS Explorer 144 Basingstoke, Alton & Whitchurch.

Refreshments There is a picnic area and barbecue site next to the play area by Lime Pits car park. Alternatively, the Bolton Arms in The Street, Old Basing welcomes children and has a large beer garden.

1 From Lime Pits car park climb up the steps on the left just before the play area. At the top, walk along the edge of the field on a gravel path. Keep to the left-hand

The Walk

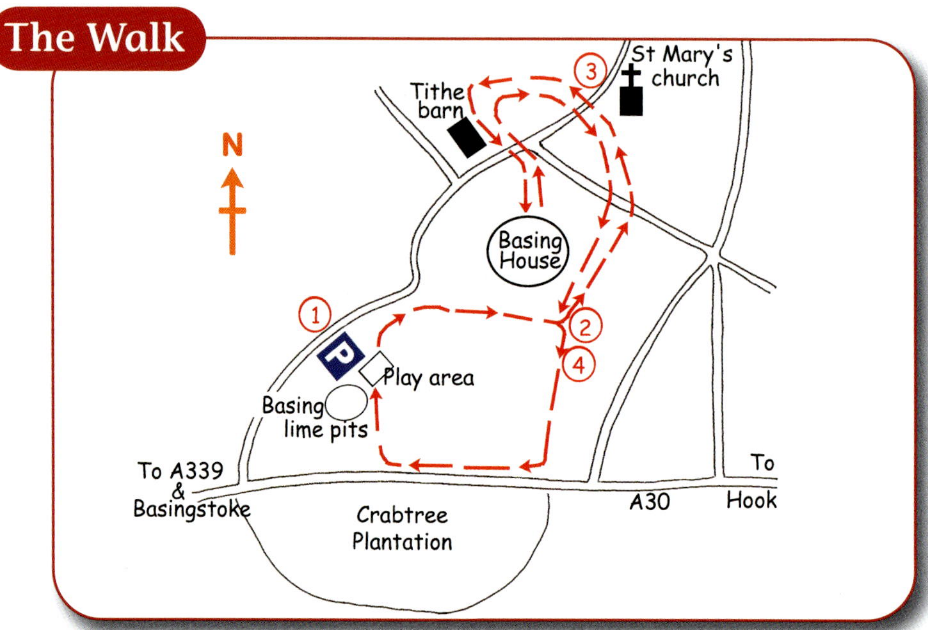

path, which takes you through a car park and kissing gate. You are now on the Basingstoke Canal Heritage Footpath. After a short walk pass through another kissing gate, continue along the left-hand side of the field and you will come to an information board on the left opposite Red Bridge. A little further on pass through another kissing gate and keep straight ahead up the field. To the left can be seen Civil War earthworks and the ruins of Basing House.

2 *To continue the shorter walk,* turn right when you reach the end of the hedge line at a junction of paths, aiming for a kissing gate at the far end, and follow the rest of the instructions for point 4. *To visit Basing House, via St Mary's church and the Great Barn,* turn left when you reach the end of the hedge line. Walk down the field, keeping the fence to your left, pass through a kissing gate and continue to the car park by Basing social club. Walk across the car park, cross the road with care and continue on the narrow footpath opposite the car park to the left of Lynwood House. At the end of the path turn left onto a lane, which leads past the church to a road.

3 Cross the road with care into Bexmoor Lane, walk past houses and continue along the narrow path until you reach the River Lodden. Turn left and walk beside the river, then after a short distance turn left again to cross a footbridge. The Tithe Barn can be seen across the field. To visit the ruins of Basing House, walk across the field and pass through a gap in the wall. Turn left and you will see the entrance to Basing House on the opposite side

◆ Fun Things to See and Do ◆

There is an excellent **children's play area** with swings, slide and climbing frame next to Lime Pits car park.

The **tithe barn** was built in 1535 and its main use was for storing grain. It bears the scars of musket and cannon balls fired during the English Civil War and is now a Scheduled Ancient Monument.

of the road. To return to the main walk, retrace your steps back to the hedge line and junction of paths (see point 2).

4 Walk straight ahead across the field, aiming for a kissing gate at the far end. When you reach the gate, turn right and walk along the edge of the field with the road to your left. Keep to the edge of the field, passing through two kissing gates. After the second kissing gate keep to the left-hand path with the hedge to your left and eventually you will see the play area and Lime Pits car park.

◆ Background Notes ◆

Basing House was built in the 16th century on the site of a Norman castle. The house was five storeys high with 380 rooms and stood within about 10 acres of land, and was the largest privately owned house in the country. The house had survived three attacks by Parliamentary troops but in the final assault in 1645 the walls were breached when Oliver Cromwell arrived with heavy artillery including a cannon which fired shot believed to have weighed between 48 and 63 pounds. Foundations and cellars of the Tudor manor are still visible and in the grounds there is a re-created Jacobean garden surrounded by Tudor walls. For opening times visit www3.hants.gov.uk/basing-house or telephone 0845 603 5635.

The **Basingstoke Canal Heritage Footpath** runs from Festival Place, the shopping centre in the centre of Basingstoke, and follows the canal to Basing House.

Crabtree Plantation, to the south of Basingstoke Common (see map), is a nature reserve with an area of open land surrounded by trees and is a popular area for kite flying and ball games. Wildlife to spot in the reserve are great spotted woodpeckers and fieldfares, brimstone butterflies and plants such as rosebay willow-herb, enchanter's nightshade and common hazel and ash trees. Entry to Crabtree Plantation from the car park is through Bolton Arch, a Grade 2 listed building, the original entrance to Hackwood Estate.

Odiham

King John's hideaway

A tranquil stretch of the Basingstoke Canal.

When you walk along this delightful stretch of the Basingstoke Canal keep an eye out for kingfishers, water voles, swans, moorhens, great crested grebes and grey herons. An extra ½ mile along the towpath from the main circular route, the ruins of Odiham Castle are well worth a visit. In Odiham village you can see the 17th-century Pest House in All Saints' churchyard which has a small museum in it.

Getting there *From junction 5 of the M3, take the A287 and follow signs for Odiham. In the village look for the 'Basingstoke Canal' sign. Continue to Odiham Wharf car park.*

Length of walk 4 miles including a visit to Odiham Castle.
Time 3 hours.
Terrain The walk is mostly on pavements and the towpath alongside Basingstoke Canal.
Start/Parking There is free parking in Odiham Wharf car park (GR 747517).

Map OS Explorer 144 Basingstoke, Alton & Whitchurch.
Refreshments There is a picnic area on the towpath near Odhiam Wharf car park. The Waterwitch, just south of the canal, is a waterside pub with a large garden and welcomes children. It also has an impressive three course children's menu. The Chequers Inn in Well is 3 miles south of Odiham. This 15th century pub has a large garden. It serves restaurant-priced food rather than pub grub. There is a large pergola at the front with a grapevine and a pretty garden.

The Walk

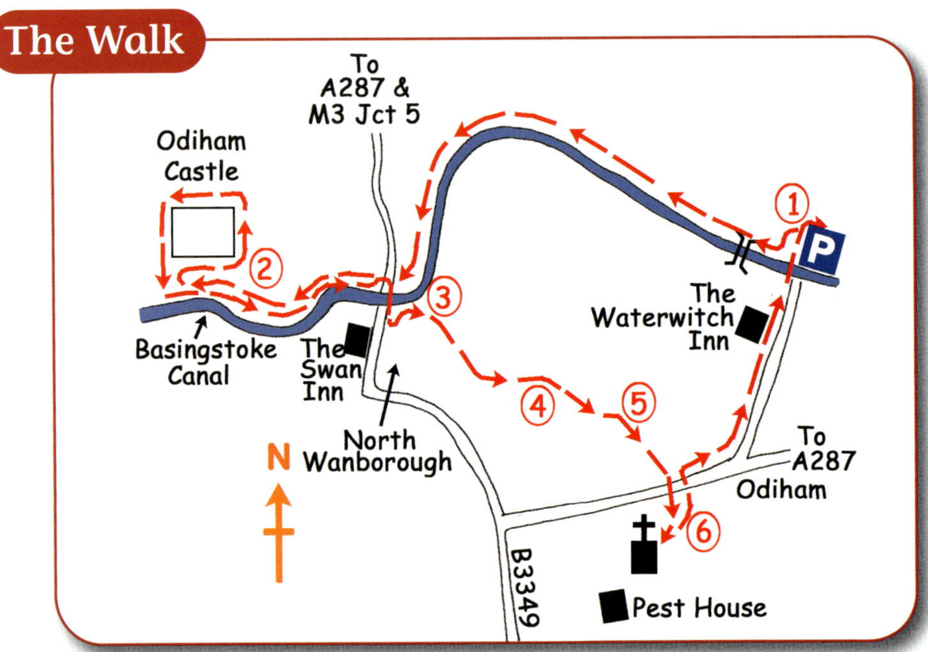

1 You can follow either path from the car park – both lead to the canal – and turn right onto the towpath. Walk past a picnic area and go under Colt Hill Bridge. Continue along the towpath for about a mile, passing a metal bridge, and then go under a low brick bridge – mind your head! Continue past another bridge, cross a road and carry on along the towpath.

2 Shortly you will see Odiham Castle on the right, which is a Scheduled Ancient Monument and a Nationally Important Archaeological Site. To continue the walk after your visit to the castle, head back to the towpath and turn left, retracing your steps back to the brick bridge. Go under the bridge and climb up steps on the left.

3 At the road turn left, and almost immediately turn left again onto a footpath. Turn next right onto a path running between houses. When you reach a road, cross over and continue straight ahead along a path through the housing estate. At the end of this path, follow a waymarked footpath along a gravel driveway then take the narrow path between hedges on the right of Deer Park Lodge.

4 Pass through a kissing gate into a field and keep left along the hedge line for a short distance. At a gap in the hedge, turn right and walk across the field, aiming for a pond surrounded by trees halfway across the field, then head for houses on the right. Walk beside a brick wall on the right; ignore the first kissing gate at the end of the wall, then after a short distance pass through the second kissing gate on the right.

◆ Fun Things to See and Do ◆

Get the children to imagine what the castle might have looked like before it fell into ruin and perhaps they can draw it when they get home.

What animals and insects can they spot near the canal? Do they know what a dragonfly looks like? There are said to be 25 different species living by the canal.

Odiham Castle was used by King John as a hunting lodge.

5 Follow the narrow path between houses to a car park. Turn right across the car park and walk past the George Hotel to the High Street. Cross over the road at the traffic lights and continue on the narrow path between the buildings ahead of you. At the end of the path turn right and very soon you will see All Saints' church. Near the entrance to the church are the village stocks and whipping post to 'encourage virtue and discourage evil doers'. To the south-west of the churchyard is the Pest House which is a Grade 2 listed building.

6 From the church, retrace your steps back to the High Street, cross over the road and turn right. Continue along the High Street, which has many attractive Grade 2 listed buildings. As the road forks, keep on the left-hand road, which eventually takes you past the Waterwitch inn on the left, and just after the bridge turn right onto a footpath; this leads back past the picnic area and the car park.

◆ Background Notes ◆

The **Basingstoke Canal**, constructed between 1788 and 1794, is 32 miles long between Greywell in Hampshire and Woodham in Surrey and has 29 locks. It was built to carry agricultural produce from Basingstoke to London. Most of the canal has been designated a Site of Special Scientific Interest and supports a wide range of aquatic plants.

Galleon Marine hires out a range of **narrrowboats** for a relaxing trip along the canal. You can also hire rowboats, kayaks, punts and canoes by the hour. For details visit www.galleonmarine.co.uk or telephone 01256 703691.

Odiham Castle was built by King John between 1207 and 1214. It was used as a hunting lodge and also a halfway house by the king on his journeys between Winchester and Windsor. Originally it would have been protected by high banks and a circular moat and the inside would have been richly decorated. In 1216 the castle was attacked by Louis the Dauphin's army. The siege lasted two weeks and the French were astounded to discover only thirteen English soldiers defending the castle.

In the churchyard of All Saints' church is a **Pest House**, built in the early 17th century. Parishioners or travellers who contracted an infectious disease, such as the plague or smallpox, would be isolated in this small single-roomed building until they recovered or died. In the late 18th century it became a poor house and was still used for this purpose until the 1930s. On display inside the building are artefacts found in the local area, including articles discovered in a Tudor well excavated in the village. The Pest House is open at weekends and bank holidays.

Hook

A country ramble

This pleasant walk is suitable for older children as a family country ramble starting from Hook, walking across fields to the pretty village of Rotherwick, which has a duck pond, an attractive village hall, a 13th-century church and the choice of two child-friendly pubs for lunch. On the return journey, look out for deer, which can often be seen in the fields.

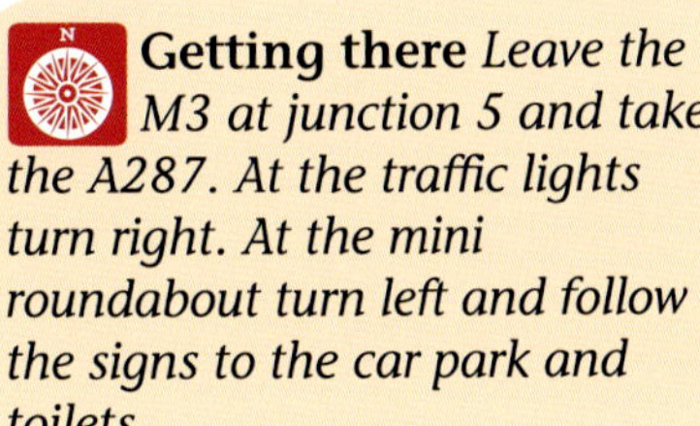

Getting there *Leave the M3 at junction 5 and take the A287. At the traffic lights turn right. At the mini roundabout turn left and follow the signs to the car park and toilets.*

Length of walk 3½ miles.
Time 1½ hours.
Terrain There is a short stretch of road walking (minor road) through Rotherwick. Two stiles.
Start/Parking Park in the pay and display car park opposite the White Hart Hotel in Hook (GR 725544).
Map OS Explorer 144 Basingstoke, Alton & Whitchurch.
Refreshments There are two child-friendly pubs in Rotherwick – the Coach and Horses has two beer gardens with ample seating; the Falcon Inn and restaurant has a grassy paddock for children to play in.

1 Turn left out of the car park opposite the White Hart Hotel and after a short distance you will see on the grass area to the left an old plough restored to its former glory by villagers and placed here in 1986 as a reminder of Hook's agricultural past. On the opposite side of the road is the parish church of St John The Evangelist, built in the 1930s. To start the walk, go back past the car park and the White Hart and continue straight ahead, cross Elms Road and pass the Old White Hart pub. Soon after turn right into Sheldons Road, which leads to a metalled footpath. Follow this path through a housing estate, crossing four roads.

2 Cross a footbridge and follow the main path, with fields to the left and a wood on the right. Ignore paths to the left and right and eventually go through a kissing gate. Turn left and walk

◆ Fun Things to See and Do ◆

Children can search for **deer prints** in the clay soil and look for **ducks** in the village pond at Rotherwick.

The Walk

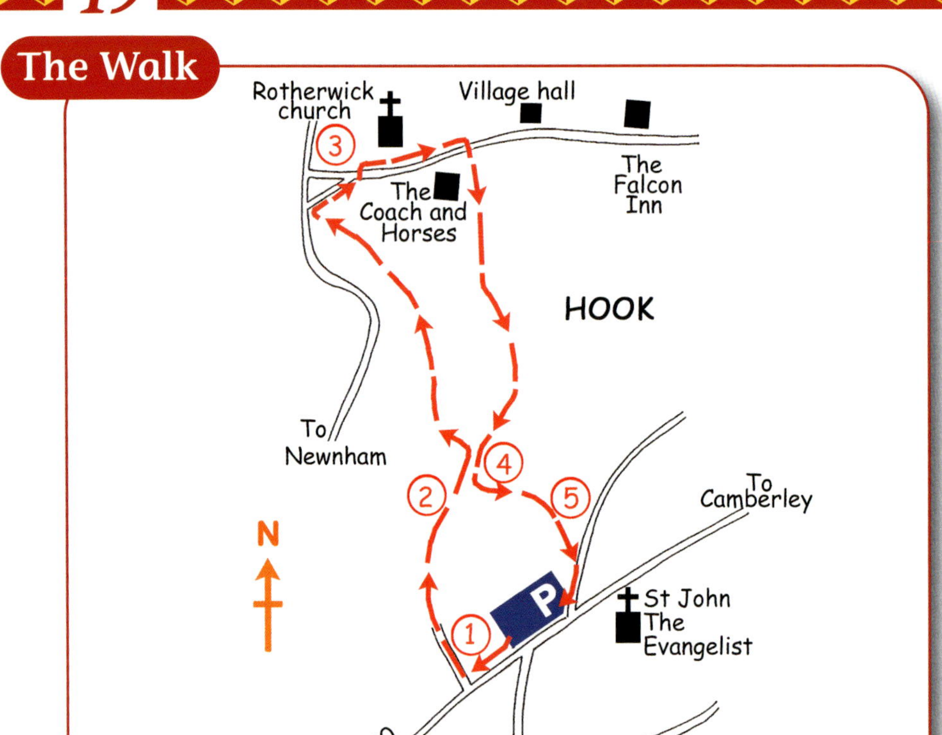

along the edge of the field; bear right around the field and go through another kissing gate and over a footbridge. Cross a track and carry on straight ahead along the edge of the field until the path bears to the left. At this point continue across the middle of the field, bearing slightly left to cross a stile, and aim for the left-hand corner of the field to cross another stile.

The imposing village hall in Rotherwick.

3 Turn right and walk a short distance along the lane into Rotherwick village then turn immediately right onto a bridleway. Follow the gravel path alongside houses and soon on the left you will see the village pond. Continue past the 13th-century parish church of Rotherwick and the Coach and Horses, then a little further on you can see the attractive village hall. Retrace your steps to a footpath just before the Coach and Horses and turn left onto a footpath. Carry on along the edge of the field and go through a kissing gate. Continue straight ahead along the hedge line, over a small footbridge and across the next field to another kissing gate. Retrace your steps by following the path, with the wood on the right, and look for a kissing gate on the left.

4 Pass through the kissing gate and walk along the edge of the wood across the field to pass through a kissing gate. Cross a shallow stream via stepping stones to the road.

5 Cross the road, bearing slightly left,and take a metalled footpath ahead between the houses. Stay on this path until you reach the road; turn right and walk back to the car park.

◆ Background Notes ◆

Hook is a large village, which developed alongside the important stagecoach route from London to Exeter. After the Second World War the village was considered as a possibility for an overspill town by London County Council, but Basingstoke was the preferred choice for the New Towns development. However, the village has grown considerably since then, especially after the M3 was built, and has now doubled in size.

St John the Evangelist church in Hook was built in the 1930s and was designed by the architect Edward Maufe who was also responsible for Guildford Cathedral. It was built to replace an iron church that was no longer adequate to serve an ever-growing community. The iron church, known as the 'tin church', had been built in the 19th century at a cost of £230 by Messrs Gowers who ran the nearby iron foundry. The church unfortunately burnt down in the 1960s.

The attractive **village hall in Rotherwick** was built in 1932 as a memorial to Charles De Forest who died of a fever aged just 24 years. Mr and Mrs De Forest, from New York, stayed at Tylney Hall in Rotherwick in the 1920s for family vacations. They enjoyed their time in the village, holding parties for their American and new-found village friends, and after Charles died they set up a charitable trust, which provided for the hall

The area to the south of Hook is a Site of Special Scientific Interest. **Hook Common and Bartley Heath** are a mixture of woodland, heathland and grassland that are home to reptiles, fungi and butterflies. **Warnborough Greens**, further south, are two wet meadows by the River Whitewater where rare early and marsh orchids can be found.

Beacon Hill

On top of the world

The iron age hill fort at the top of Beacon Hill.

If your children have excess energy to burn, then a race up Beacon Hill followed by a scramble up and down the ramparts should do the trick. There are spectacular views from the top, where you can point out Highclere Castle, this Victorian castle is instantly recognisable as *Downton Abbey*, where the successful TV series was filmed. The surrounding countryside includes Highclere Stud and Watership Down, the area where rabbits set up their warren in Richard Adams' famous novel. Don't miss the grave of the 5th Earl of Carnarvon, which is sited on top of the hill. In 1922 Howard Carter and the Earl discovered King Tutankhamun's Tomb on an expedition to Egypt's Valley of the Kings. Also you can get the children to look for evidence of Iron Age life within the banks, where storage pits and the site of hut circles can be seen.

20

Getting there *From the A34 follow the brown tourist signs for Beacon Hill and Highclere Castle. Turn left at the sign for Highclere Stud, then turn immediately left again into the road that leads to Beacon Hill car park. Approaching from the north, take the B4640 and exit towards Newtown/Burghclere. Take the second exit at the roundabout and turn right to White Hill and then sharp right to pick up the brown tourist signs to Beacon Hill.*

Length of walk 1½ miles.
Time 1 hour.

Terrain The climb up to the top of Beacon Hill is steep, but well worth the effort. It is a grassy track and there are steps to climb at some points along the way.
Start/Parking Beacon Hill car park (GR 463577).
Map OS Explorer 144 Basingstoke, Alton & Winchester.
Refreshments There is a picnic site next to the car park – or enjoy your picnic at the top of the hill overlooking the Hampshire countryside. The Swan Inn, Newtown, just south of Newbury is family-friendly with outside seating and children's menus.

The Walk

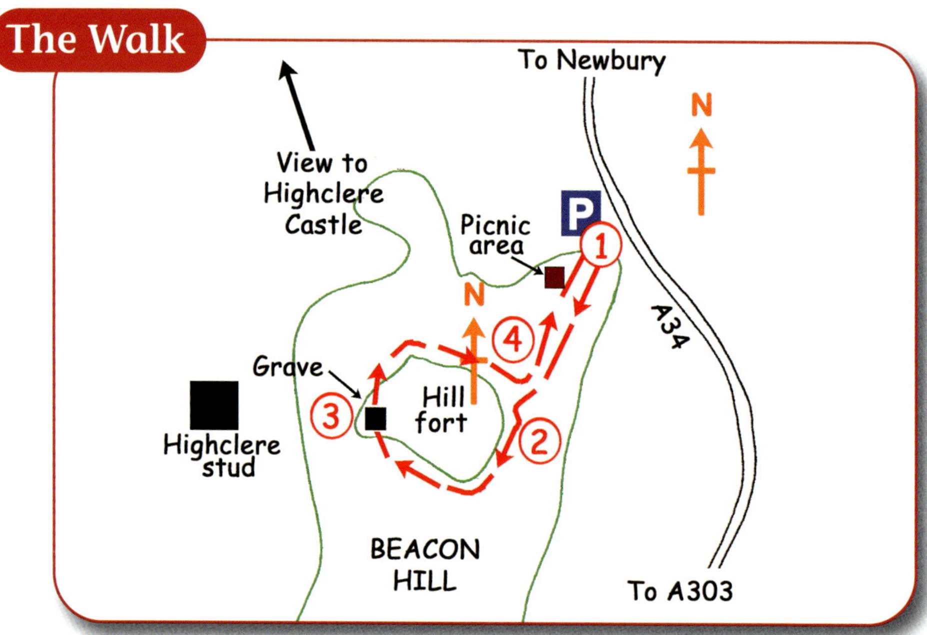

1 Follow the path to the left of a picnic area and start the climb to the top of the hill. Keep straight ahead and carry on up the steps. Pass through a kissing gate and continue up the hill. Highclere Castle can be seen in the distance on your right, a good excuse to stop and catch your breath while admiring the fantastic views.

2 When you reach the ramparts of the Iron Age hill fort, turn left and continue on the outer rampart. Ignore a kissing gate on the left and keep to the outer rampart.

3 After a short while you will see a fenced off area which contains the grave of George

Following the path to the top of the hill.

Edward Stanhope Molyneux, the 5th Earl of Carnarvon. Highclere Stud, founded by the Earl in 1902, can be seen on the left in the valley. Continue on the outer ramparts.

4 Pass a trig point and turn left retracing your steps down the well-marked path. In the distance you can see the earthworks of an unfinished hill fort on Ladle Hill. A little further on past this hill

◆ Fun Things to See and Do ◆

This is a good place for **wildflower spotting** – in the summer months you can see clustered bellflower, rock-rose, kidney vetch and wild thyme. A rare solitary bee, the Osmia bicolour, feeds on bird's foot trefoil, a plant that also flourishes on the hill.

fort is Watership Down, made famous by Richard Adams' novel about rabbits setting up a warren on the Down. Retrace your steps down the hill past the picnic area and back to the car park.

◆ Background Notes ◆

Beacon Hill is a Site of Special Scientific Interest, a National Nature Reserve and was the site of the most famous beacon in Hampshire. The last beacon was lit on 2nd June 1977, the Queen's Silver Jubilee. The chalk grassland habitat on the hill is grazed by sheep, which helps to keep down the scrub and allows chalk loving flowers to thrive.

Highclere Stud: Henry George Reginald Molyneux Herbert, the 7th Earl of Carnarvon, was racing manager to Queen Elizabeth II.

To the south of Beacon Hill in Seven Barrows field, is the **de Havilland flight memorial**. Geoffrey de Havilland was an aeroplane designer, founder of an aircraft company and pioneer aviator and made his first successful flight from here on 10th September 1910.

You could combine your walk on Beacon Hill with a visit to **Highclere Castle**, a Victorian country house set in beautiful parkland – said to be the largest mansion in Hampshire. The castle is now famous as the fictional 'Downton Abbey', home to the Earl and Countess of Grantham and their servants. In reality, this spot has been the ancestral home of the Carnarvon family since 1679. The present Earl and Countess of Carnarvon still live here and have been known to take tea in the tearoom. In 1922, the 5th Earl of Carnarvon and Howard Carter discovered the Tomb of the Egyptian Boy Pharaoh, Tutankhamun. There is a fascinating Egyptian Exhibition in the castle's cellars. Since the filming of *Downton Abbey*, the place has become incredibly popular with visitors, with pre-booked tickets always all sold out. See the website for details of prices, visiting times and how to get on-the-day tickets: www.highclerecastle.co.uk.